Creative

es

ry

for

CY

for

Creative Approaches to Poetry

for the Primary Framework for

LITERACY

Jan Foale and Linda Pagett

Routledge
Taylor & Francis Group

LONDON AND NEW YORK

First published 2009
by Routledge
2 Park Square, Milton Park, Abingdon, Oxon, OX14 4RN

Simultaneously published in the USA and Canada
by Routledge
270 Madison Avenue, New York, NY 10016

Routledge is an imprint of the Taylor & Francis Group, an informa business

© 2009 Jan Foale and Linda Pagett

Typeset in Celeste and Bliss by
Florence Production Ltd, Stoodleigh, Devon
Printed and bound in Great Britain by
The Cromwell Press, Trowbridge, Wiltshire

British Library Cataloguing in Publication Data
A catalogue record for this book is available from the British Library

Library of Congress Cataloging in Publication Data
Foale, Jan.
    Creative approaches to poetry for the primary framework for
    literacy / Jan Foale and Linda Pagett.
        p. cm.
    Includes bibliographical references.
        1. Poetry – Study and teaching (Elementary)   2. Language arts
(Elementary)   I. Pagett, Linda.   II. Title.
LB1575.F63 2008
372.64 – dc22   2008004728

ISBN10: 0–415–46265–7 (pbk)
ISBN13: 978–0–415–46265–5 (pbk)

Contents

Illustrations

Figures

Plates

Preface

Poetry is powerful. Why? Because poets write cleverly. They carefully choose words so that they chime together. They strip words away leaving us an essence of language, concentrated and heady. Poems often make an important point and the voice within them beguiles us. We want to listen, we want to hear it again and again, and finally we may want to write poetry ourselves.

The curriculum acknowledges the importance of poetry and the revised Primary Framework for Literacy (Department for Education and Skills (DfES), 2006) suggests a model for planning units of poetry work. Our book builds on the suggested plans for Key Stage 1 (KS 1) and Foundation stage pupils, giving poems and activities that could help children to engage as readers, writers and presenters. In order to ensure that the suggestions are successful we worked with early years school teachers to plan and teach seven poems. On occasions the teachers decided to adapt our plans for their own classes and their own interests, and we have included these adaptations in the form of photographs, teachers' comments and examples of children's work. What we offer here are suggestions for planning and teaching, which could be adapted creatively to suit a range of different teaching contexts. We suggest a model for teaching poetry and trust you will find it useful. We do hope you enjoy teaching poetry as much as we do and that your pupils engage as intensely as the children in our project.

Jan Foale
Linda Pagett

Acknowledgements

We would like to thank the many people who helped to make this book: the staff and pupils at Exminster Community Primary School, especially Headteacher Bob Foale and teachers Annie Fletcher, Gail Miller, Bridget Oliver, Ian Moore and Sarah Phillips. Thanks also to Tony Ovens from the University of Exeter, who took the photographs. Their patience, energy, generosity and creativity are tributes to the work undertaken in school.

We are grateful to the following who have kindly granted permission for the use of copyright material:

'Rumble in the Jungle' from *Rumble in the Jungle* by Giles Andreae, first published in the UK by Orchard Books, a division of the Watts Publishing Group Ltd, 338, Euston Road, London NW1 3BH.

'The Bag' by Tony Mitton from *Plum*, reprinted with permission from David Higham Associates.

'Rhyme' by Elizabeth Coatsworth reprinted with permission from the author.

'Dragon' by Jean Kenward reprinted with permission from the author.

'Walking with my Iguana' from *Behind the Staffroom Door: The Best of Brian Moses* (Macmillan, 2008), © Brian Moses.

'Snail' by Ted Hughes from *The Cat and the Cuckoo*, permission granted by Faber & Faber Ltd, © Ted Hughes Estate.

'Giant Upstairs' by Stanley Cook, permission granted by Sarah Matthews, © The estate of Stanley Cook.

Abbreviations

DfES	Department for Education and Skills
EAL	English as an additional language
ICT	information and communication technology
IWB	interactive whiteboard
KS 1	Key Stage 1
NLS	National Literacy Strategy
PGCE	Post Graduate Certificate in Education
PHSE	Personal, Health and Social Education
QCA	Qualifications and Curriculum Authority

CHAPTER 1

Poetry, young learners and the curriculum

The Poetry Club

Poetry is important. Some people know this: poets, musicians, songwriters, people who invent advertising jingles are all in the Poetry Club. Harry is a member too. He sits in bed with his parents singing: 'There was an old lady who swallowed a fly . . .' He is only two but like many young children he is beginning to pick up the rhythm of nursery rhymes and even to manipulate rhyme himself: he calls his younger sister 'Liz the Fizz'. The Club encompasses everyone who enjoys listening to poetry. Some people, like Harry, get membership early because they have people to help them: people who introduce them to a wonderful world, where language is easy to memorise, where phrases stay with them in a way that prose may not. Harry remembers the phrase 'fearful earful', which describes the sound of elephants trumpeting, from his story book. He laughs when he says it. As his understanding increases he may use it as a phrase to describe any loud noise, thus enriching his own use of language. Some members of the Club enjoy writing poetry but these are few and far between. There are some closet members who may write poetry to help them to understand life a little better, but how many adults admit to this?

Sadly, not everyone joins the Club. Some people just don't experience enough poetry; others are actually rather scared, thinking it difficult to understand and write. Some of these people may be teachers, and this is really quite serious. Kelly argues that historically, 'some children enjoyed their teacher's passion for poetry, while others were at the mercy of their teacher's indifference' (2005: 129). She analyses contemporary children's views about poetry and finds that, 'despite their years of poetry teaching, these children still indicate that poetry and poets inhabit a privileged place where they do not belong' (2005: 132). This is a challenge to the most dedicated of teachers and underlines the difficulties in keeping up your Club subscription.

How do we join?

Membership depends upon what Frank Smith (1971) famously called the company we keep. Harry's Mum sings with him and takes him to a music club where parents and children sing together, march up and down and dance as only two year olds can. The children in the music class need others around them to stay enthusiastic about poetry and to continue to create contexts in which they can respond. They are lucky. Others may need to wait until they get to school before they are introduced to poetry. There they may learn from their peers, for example, chanting and clapping together in the playground, and hopefully from teachers who are enthusiastic about poetry, weaving it into the fabric of the school day. There will, of course, be reluctant members; perhaps children who feel themselves to be poor readers and writers and so unable to access poetic form for themselves; perhaps clever children who are expected to analyse and comb through poems exhaustively in the name of 'comprehension'. Poems themselves can convert you into a Club member, catching you unaware, creeping into your memory, perhaps making you wonder. Ted Hughes claims that poems 'have a certain wisdom. They know something special' (Hughes, 1967: 15). It is perhaps this wisdom that makes it so important for young children to be switched onto poetry.

How teachers can help

Teachers themselves need to be in the Club. This is not an automatic attribute of being a teacher. I recently asked a group of PGCE students about their attitudes to teaching poetry. Their comments varied from the dramatic 'complete dread' through 'nervous and a bit embarrassed' to 'enthusiastic'. One comment was particularly telling: 'Before school experience complete dread! Now I can't wait till the next opportunity.' Working with children and poetry can be a catalyst for change, empowering both teachers and pupils.

However, teachers may need to 'find a friend' in order to help them. This may be an alliance with a colleague interested in other art forms: dance or drama, for example. Balaam and Merrick (1987) report inspiring case studies into how children can use various art forms in order to explore and enjoy poems. Research undertaken by Medwell *et al.* (1998) has shown that the most effective teachers of literacy have an extensive knowledge of children's literature, so having colleagues who are constantly sharing and comparing poems to teach children is important.

How the curriculum helps

The Education Act of 1986 heralded the arrival of a National Curriculum for English. It came with a requirement for all pupils to be given opportunities to speak aloud, listen to and discuss poetry, to read a range of poems and to write their own. The commitment to poetry remained in the National Literacy Strategy (NLS) (DfES, 1998) and the Curriculum Guidance for the Foundation Stage (DfEE, 2000). Unfortunately, documentation that stipulates an entitlement to poetry is no guarantee of effective teaching or learning. Why is this so? Perhaps the answer lies in pedagogy.

With the NLS came the literacy hour, which prescribed shared, guided and independent work within a sixty minute lesson. Poems provided concise texts well-suited to analysis at word and sentence level. Poetry found a place in the hour but perhaps lost its connection to the wider curriculum; the power of poetry was sometimes diminished, and as a result some poetry enthusiasts lost their way.

However, the Primary National Strategy (DfES, 2003), with its clear mandate to excellence and enjoyment, has provided teachers with the timely encouragement to be creative and innovative in their interpretation of the curriculum. Teachers are invited to use their professional judgement and knowledge of children to make choices about how best to serve their pupils' needs. In the case of poetry this may mean more variety. Free from the restraints of the literacy hour, poetry can be explored via pen and paint, music and mime, dance and drama, **performance** and **presentation** – and it can be linked to the wider curriculum.

Early learning goals included in Early Years Foundation Stage Communication Language and Literacy (DfES, 2007) underline the importance of poetry for young children. The learning goals include 'listen with enjoyment and respond to . . . rhymes and poems and make up their own' (2007: 13) and 'enjoy listening to and using spoken and written language and readily turn to it in their play' (2007: 13).

The Primary Framework for Literacy (DfES, 2006) draws upon the National Literacy Strategy and Curriculum Guidance for the Foundation Stage. The following KS 1 models for planning taken from the Primary Framework underline the significance of poetry alongside narrative and non-fiction. Furthermore, the Framework suggests that the units of work extend over a period of one to two weeks, enabling connections to be explored progressively. Each unit has a suggested theme. Themes have been chosen to provide variety in terms of the types of poetry and subject matter likely to motivate young learners. This book is designed to support teachers who are working within and beyond these suggested models.

A sequence for progression

If we are serious about the quality of pupils' learning, we need to think carefully about progression. The five stage sequence below – paving the way; meeting the poem; presenting and performing; reflecting, reading and writing around the poem and becoming a poet – is a suggested approach that can be used alongside the

Year 1 Poetry

Narrative 16–17 weeks	UNIT 1 **Stories with familiar settings** (4 weeks or 2 × 2 weeks)	UNIT 2 **Stories from a range of cultures/stories with predictable and patterned language** (4 weeks or 2 × 2 weeks)	UNIT 3 **Traditional and fairy tales (includes plays)** (4–5 weeks or 2–3 + 2 weeks)	UNIT 4 **Stories about fantasy worlds** (4 weeks or 2 × 2 weeks)
Non-fiction 12 weeks	UNIT 1 **Labels, lists and captions** (1 week)	UNIT 2 **Instructions** (2 weeks)	UNIT 3 **Recounts, dictionary** (2 weeks)	UNIT 4 **Information texts** (5 weeks)	UNIT 4 **Information texts** (5 weeks)
Poetry 6 weeks	UNIT 1 **Using the senses*** (2 weeks)		UNIT 2 **Pattern and rhyme** (2 weeks)		UNIT 3 **Poems on a theme** (2 weeks)

Figure 1.1 Year 1 Poetry.

Source: Department for Children, Schools and Families. Reproduced under the terms of the Click Use License.

Year 2 Poetry

Narrative 14 weeks	UNIT 1 **Stories with familiar settings** (4 weeks)	UNIT 2 **Traditional stories** (4 weeks)	UNIT 3 **Different stories by the same author** (3 weeks)	UNIT 4 **Extended stories/ Significant authors** (3 weeks)
Non-fiction 15 weeks	UNIT 1 **Instructions** (4 weeks)	UNIT 2 **Explanations** (3 weeks)	UNIT 3 **Information texts** (4 weeks)	UNIT 4 **Non-chronological reports** (4 weeks)
Poetry 6 weeks	UNIT 1 **Patterns on the page** (2 weeks)		UNIT 2 **Really looking** (2 weeks)		UNIT 3 **Silly stuff** (2 weeks)

Figure 1.2 Year 2 Poetry.

Source: Department for Children, Schools and Families. Reproduced under the terms of the Click Use License.

Primary Framework for Literacy. Teachers may choose to follow the whole sequence or simply focus on particular stages such as presenting and performing.

Poems can be used in a variety of ways; for example, there may be a reading or recitation of a new poem at registration time, which stands alone. It takes only a few moments of the school day but it is there to build upon children's existing repertoires of poetic work. Alternatively, a teacher may choose to extend the learning opportunities from a particular poem in any of the following ways.

Paving the way

Some poems have an immediate appeal to children, whilst others need to be introduced by adults as children might initially dismiss them as being too difficult or not for them. Activities that provide meaningful contexts, support investigation and activate children's prior experience and knowledge are important. Such activities may make a difference to a poem being embraced or rejected. For example, a teacher about to read 'Bully Night' by Roger McGough (1983) to their class might choose to explore the meanings of the word 'bully'. This might take the form of drama or class discussion, directly linked to children's own lives and related to PHSE (Personal, Health and Social Education).

Meeting the poem

Simply reading a poem is no guarantee of engagement. The poem can be 'met' in various ways; for example, by encouraging children to draw or make models in response. Poems are often not illustrated, which leaves a wide margin for children's imagination. The pictures in their head can be sharpened and misconceptions addressed simply by drawing. Figure 1.3 shows a pupil's response to the poem 'My Other Granny' by Ted Hughes (1988). The lines: 'When the world rolls blind as a boulder in the night-sea surf' are challenging in terms of metaphoric comprehension as the image could only be viewed from outer space. The child's drawing captures perfectly the energy of the world, flinging off the sea creatures as it rolls dramatically in an astral ocean.

Figure 1.3 A drawing of 'The World Rolls Blind As a Boulder in the Night Sea Surf'.

Drawing is only one form of visualisation; it can take place in the mind as we read or hear a poem and be interpreted through drama strategies such as **freeze frame**, **tableau** and **white mime**.

Devising and making drama enables children to get inside the poem, exploring issues and understanding characters, settings, mood and atmosphere. Drama in education can take many forms. It can be taught because it is a recognised art form, an important strand of speaking and listening as identified by the National Curriculum (DfEE, 1999), and as a relevant strategy to support cross curricular links. Winston and Tandy describe drama as a 'cultural activity which brings together these two human propensities for play and story telling' (2001: vii). Young children are programmed to play; it is the way in which they come to understand the world around them. While children 'play' with impossible notions, such as becoming a cabbage (see Chapter 7), drama strategies support their understanding of the cabbage's point of view. Such imaginative and enjoyable play can be demanding as participants need to be able to internalise ideas and consider them from a variety of perspectives.

Stories are the means by which we all learn to live. As humans we do not seem to be able to manage without narrative forms. Barbara Hardy (1977: 12) described narrative as 'a primary act of mind', meaning that we use story to recount our lives both to ourselves and to others: what is happening, what has happened and what might happen in the future. While we do this we try to make sense of strange, new, inspiring or troubling occurrences, rehearsing, dreaming about and some-times agonising over what might be.

Poems often tell a story, or connect with other stories. Using drama, we can create other stories around the original text. In Chapter 8 we use the poem 'Walking With My Iguana', in which Brian Moses narrates a story about taking his pet iguana for a stroll. By using **hot seating** we are able to create other stories: the story of the bystander; what she thinks of such an exotic pet; the story of the iguana, and how he came to be walking along a beach in Hastings. The oral story form can then be transcribed without the curse of the reluctant writer who does not know what to write. The drama has helped the children to compose their story long before they begin transcription.

Discussion supports listening, responding, raising questions and searching for meaning. Questions are important and can be framed thoughtfully by the teacher. They help us to infer, to deduce and to consider the 'What ifs', entering a world of exciting possibilities. Encouraging children to raise their own questions is important; simply using an enlarged text of 'Jack and Jill' can elicit questions such as: 'Why are they going up the hill?' 'Who are Jack and Jill?' 'Why did Jack fall down?' Readers need to be active if they are to comprehend texts, and this involves engaging with the whole text rather than puzzling over what individual words mean. You can be ambitious with your choice of poem. In Chapter 4 we use the poem 'The Bag' by Tony Mitton. This has some challenging vocabulary for Year 1 children, including 'rue' and 'thyme'. However, the teacher with whom we worked was happy with this. She used real examples of herbs in her drama work, which ensured that all the children were engaged with the meaning as participants in the story.

Presenting and performing

We all learn in different ways. Some of us learn best by doing, so making a model in response to the poem can deepen understanding. Alternatively, children may draw characters or settings from poems; they may also choose to recite or to sing, and these can be recorded in various ways. The example in Figure 1.4 demonstrates how information and communication technology (ICT) can be used to record work. Children were introduced to 'The Pied Piper of Hamlyn' by Robert Browning. After experimenting with various ways of reading the poem, they made drawings of what they considered to be important scenes. This involved returning to the text in order to understand significant details. The children then recorded their own voices reciting the work as part of a multimedia presentation.

Figure 1.4 A slide from a PowerPoint presentation of *The Pied Piper of Hamlyn*, in which the children provided a reading of the poem and some drawings.

Source: Pagett and Somers, 2004: 61.

Reading, writing and reflecting

Writing can help us to think: it gives us time to reflect as we struggle to compose what we want to say. Writing around poetry can include:

- writing in role as a character in the poem;

- exchanging the genre, such as writing a prose version of the original work;

- making word collages, which take original words and phrases from poems and illustrate them;

- describing your own response for others, for example a poetry review;

- reading and writing profiles of poets and their work, and

- making timelines of narrative poems.

This roaming around the poem can provide opportunities for further reflection and encourage children to find new forms of writing for themselves.

Reading around the poem can involve:

- reading other poems by the same poet for comparison;

- reading other poems on the same theme (some suggestions are given at the end of each chapter); and

- relating previous reading to the poem being studied. This is an important context for developing an understanding of intertextuality in the young reader. In Chapter 5 we use the poem 'Dragon' by Jean Kenward with children who extended what they already knew about dragons from films, animations and stories. These related texts were spontaneously brought to school to be shared with others.

Becoming a poet

Becoming a poet is the final mastery over poetic form. The previous stages of the sequence can inspire writing so that children are drawing upon a rich artistic experience in order to sharpen their understanding of poetry in its various forms.

Some children who are immersed in poetry will spontaneously begin to write. Others need scaffolding for their writing to support the journey that ideas have to make from our heads to paper. This can take many forms: concept mapping; using poetry games; shared, paired and guided writing, and using texts as models. Careful assessment of children's poems can provide evidence of sophisticated knowledge and understanding of poetry. For example, a Year 1 pupil wrote an acrostic poem in response to the 'Dragon':

Down in the glittering swimming pool,
Runs a dragon breathing fire
And eating people,
Groaning and moaning
On a boat
Near a dragon nest.

(The spellings have been corrected here). This pupil is able to use poetic language ('glittering'); she manipulates time well by writing in the present tense ('runs a dragon'); she uses rhyme ('groaning and moaning') and alliteration ('near a dragon nest'), and she is able to add descriptive phrases ('breathing fire'). She understands narration, setting the scene with the line: 'Down in the glittering swimming pool', and is able to add her own understanding of fantasy, inventing a 'dragon nest'. If the teacher shares all of these strengths with the children by using a meta-cognitive approach (such as 'I really like the way you use an interesting word like "glittering"'), this can further extend their understanding of poetic form.

If you are a teacher who is passionate about poetry or a teacher whose subscription to the Poetry Club has lapsed a little, if your shelves at home are groaning with poetry books or if you feel as though you may need a few ideas to support your interest in poetry teaching, this book may help you to put together a sequence for teaching poetry in all its dimensions: reading, writing, performing and presenting.

CHAPTER 2

Poetry in the Foundation Stage

The NLS (DfES, 1998) introduced shared reading and the use of big books into many early years' classrooms. These enlarged texts are useful for the teacher to model reading processes such as anticipation ('I wonder what's on the next page . . .') and understanding of concepts of print such as directionality ('point to the words as we say them'). All this can be achieved while maintaining the intimacy of a whole class read, an important consideration in any early years' setting. Andreae's episodic poem 'Rumble in the Jungle' is available as a big book, dramatically illustrated with the vibrant colours of an imaginary jungle.

Rumble in the Jungle

There's a rumble in the jungle,
There's a whisper in the trees,
The animals are waking up
And rustling the leaves.

The hippo's at the Waterhole,
The leopard's in his lair,
The chimpanzees are chattering
And swinging everywhere.

Some animals are frightening,
And some are sweet and kind,
So let's go to the jungle now
And see who we can find . . .

It's great to be a chimpanzee,
Swinging through the trees
And if we can't find nuts to eat
We munch each other's fleas!

The lion's the king of the jungle
Just listen how loudly he roars!
Every animal quivers
And shudders and shivers
As soon as he opens his jaws.

It's great to be an elephant
All big and fat and round,
And wander through the jungle
Just elephing around.

The boa constrictor's a slippery snake
Who slithers and slides round his tree,
And when tasty animals wander too close
He squashes them slowly for tea.

Hello, I'm a big happy hippo
I sleep in the sun to get hot,
And when I'm not sleeping
I mooch in the mud,
Which hippos like doing a lot.

The night has started falling
But the jungle never sleeps,
The vultures circle slowly
While the leopard softly creeps.

And if you listen quietly
You might just hear the growl
Of a hungry pair of panthers,
Who are still out on the prowl.

The lions and their little cubs
Are sleeping in their den,
So let's leave them till tomorrow
When we'll visit them again.

(Andreae, 1996)

This narrative has an immediate attraction for young language users. The subject matter dealing with the characteristics of jungle animals is likely to resonate with a young child's world. It is likely that many children will be familiar with some, if not all, of the animals in the poem. Whether or not children have first hand experience, it is likely, given the popularity of animal images in our society, that jungle creatures appear on their wallpaper, bedclothes, T-shirts, birthday cards and even on some of their favourite food and drink cartons. Add to this the plethora of cuddly soft toys, picture books, television wildlife programmes and cartoons, which all portray animals, and the scene is set for close engagement.

The first three verses introduce the story with a clever play on words. The near-rhyme of 'rumble' and 'jungle' and the alliteration in 'chimpanzees . . . chattering' and the 'leopard in his lair' are all teasing to the ear. The rhythm is established early on in the work and encourages anticipation of the next words and stanzas. Further verses then introduce each of the animals to be found in the jungle (eleven are published here), which include memorable phrases such as 'gangly giraffe' and the occasional invented word such as 'elphing around'. The last three verses then quietly bring the poem to a close. There is an invitation to introduce mood and atmosphere into the stanzas. The verse describing the snake for instance, which begins: 'The boa constrictor's a slippery snake', can be whispered quietly with just a hint of menace; whereas the verse that introduces the hippo, 'Hello, I'm a big happy hippo', can be read in a lazy, indolent kind of way. There are also wonderful opportunities here for using musical instruments, for example, a shaker to accompany the words 'whisper in the trees', and each of the animal verses can be performed by individuals 'in role' as animals.

A poem such as this, with its strong visual cues and an invitation for choral work, is an ideal context for the child with EAL (English as an additional language). In her important research with early-stage learners of English, Drury (2007) stresses the importance of providing opportunities for joining in choral responses and ensuring that the learners are made to feel part of a group, 'even when the linguistic context is beyond their full understanding, and accepting their non-verbal response' (p. 104). Listening to and perhaps using musical instruments or puppets to accompany works such as this are important non-threatening opportunities for group work and effective listening.

Paving the way

- Take the class to a zoo or safari park to see some of the animals in the poem first-hand or show high-quality photographic images. Discuss animals' appearance, habitat and so on.

- Play a guessing game; for example, 'I'm a very lazy cat with big claws and I like roaring. Who am I?' This introduces **riddles**. See if children can find the appropriate illustration in the book.

- Have fun playing this animal game. You will need matching pairs of pictures depicting different animals. Each child is secretly given a picture of an animal and has to find, by sound and action, the child hiding the same animal picture that they have. Cards can be reshuffled and the game repeated. Prepare yourself and other colleagues for a noisy ten minutes!

Meeting the poem

- Read the first three verses using the Big Book or an interactive whiteboard (IWB) by pointing to each word.

- If using the Big Book, draw children's attention to the illustrations. Can they guess what the animals are from the tails, ears and so on, glimpsed through the grass or behind trees?

- Read through the verses leaving out the animal names and then ask children if they can guess what animal it is.

- As you read each verse try to create different voices for each animal by altering the pitch and tone. Alternatively, elicit the support of other adults to share the verses and the voices.

- Use an open space such as the hall and set off in front of the children as their 'jungle guide'. To support your control of the situation explain that they will all need to follow you and your instructions in order to 'stay safe'.

- Lead them across the space by describing how they might move as if in a jungle – stepping over tree roots, pushing through vines, creeping past a sleeping lion and so on. This can be done with small groups or the whole class depending on available adults and the type of early years' setting. This journey can be repeated incorporating the children's own suggestions.

- Either in this situation or during the **imaginative play**, an adult might use the drama strategy of **teacher in role** – for example, becoming an explorer and asking for the children's help to photograph or track down a wounded animal. Taking on the **low status role** of someone needing help can often produce amazing involvement from the children.

Presenting and performing

- Choose some of the children to practise an animal verse on their own. They may need help with this; one technique that you can use is to read with them and then ask them to read the last line independently, the last two lines independently and so on.

- Children who might find the above approach difficult can work in a group learning only the three first introductory and final verses together. The teacher reads the verses in between.

- If you don't have time for rote learning, an alternative is for the teacher to read the first and last three verses, with the children joining in for only the last line of each. As you read, one child (possibly wearing an animal **mask** or face paint) can pretend to be the animal with appropriate actions. It is helpful for the children to stand in line as this helps them remember their cue. Finally, perform with as many or few of the animal verses as you like.

Plate 2.1 Making animal masks.

- To enhance a performance to an audience, make animal masks or alternatively organise some face painting. The addition of masks or face paint supports getting into role and can be a real incentive for children to join in the poem when it is 'their' animal. For health and safety reasons, this has to be done by an adult with appropriate materials.

- Listening to a rhyme or piece of music is rarely done passively. Children need to move, clap their hands, wave their arms and jump around. The rhythm becomes a whole body experience. In order for children to experience the poem kinaesthetically, you may wish to dramatise the animals in the poem through movement and music. This work could then be incorporated into a performance, as suggested above.

- Young children generally have few inhibitions when invited to 'become animals', although their initial movements may entail dashing around on all fours. By selecting key qualities of the animals as described in the poem, the children may be encouraged to work on some more focused movement. For example, the children might move like the vultures circling slowly or the leopards as they slowly creep.

- Select some suitable music for each of the animals or work on your own musical accompaniment with tuned or untuned instruments. A collection of the latter could be explored freely with the children deciding which instrument would best suit each animal and how that instrument would need to be played.

Reading, writing and reflecting

Although many young children will be familiar with images and ideas associated with wild animals (and a suggested visit to a zoo will support this), children need to explore a jungle within the context of their imaginative play. In this way they begin to make sense of the new and unfamiliar, perhaps even the frightening. Children may be seen to do this spontaneously within a playground context or you might support this imaginative exploration by introducing a role play area. If you are fortunate enough to have an outside area with trees and grass, you could simply provide a box of **props**, which might contain safari style clothing, water bottles, cameras, binoculars, specimen-collecting jars and so on. Pop-up tents and sleeping bags are useful and the former can be put up easily by young children. You could add soft toys such as snakes to hang from the trees or leave this to the children's imaginations.

If you are not able to provide a role play area you might, with the children's help, decorate a corner of the class space to depict a jungle. Complete this with paper vines, tropical flowers and a tent to sit in and you have created a stimulating setting in which children can browse through high-quality fiction and non-fiction texts. These can include appropriate illustrations and photographs of jungle animals and stories.

Becoming a poet

Young children delight in playing with words. However, it is likely that they will need support with both the composition and transcription processes when capturing this wordplay on paper or screen.

- Using the large outline of an animal, scribe descriptive words suggested by the children inside the shape. This could be a whole class or small group activity and lead to individual work as appropriate.

- Use the words from the above work to make phrases or sentences. These could be written around an animal outline.

- Using the model below, add and change the bold lines according to the children's suggestions and sing the verses to the tune of Frere Jacque:

> In the jungle
> In the jungle
> We can see
> We can see
> **Lions leaping**
> **Lions leaping**
> Wild and free
> Wild and free

How it worked in the classroom

The foundation class first enjoyed a day at a local zoo. When we visited their school they had already 'met' the poem, and talked about the zoo animals they had seen that also featured in the rhyme. An interesting discussion had taken place in relation to the freedom of animals living in a jungle compared to those living in captivity. Some children thought animals would be better off roaming in a jungle whereas others felt some animals would be better off in a zoo, protected from their enemies while enjoying meals that they didn't have to catch!

As the class included a significant number of children with special educational needs, there were two teachers and a number of learning support assistants to support a performance of part of the poem.

In preparation for their poetry performance, the children were divided into groups and each group was allocated a specific animal. When we became their audience, the children had already rehearsed their allocated verses and made face masks. The groups practised their presentation, adding mime and adapting their voices according to the attributes of the animal they were presenting. The groups had been chosen to represent a balance of gender and ability. Some of the children, who were unable to memorise the words, were able to use action or musical instruments.

Following the first performance, the teacher asked the children to repeat it so that he could record the recitation. This served to add a real sense of audience and supported focused work, uninterrupted by background noise. The teacher intended to use this recording with small groups at a later date to support their reflection both of the poem and of their performance. He might alternatively have filmed their performances.

Related outcomes from the Primary Framework for Literacy for Foundation Stage

Speaking

Enjoy listening to and using spoken and written language and readily turn to it in play and learning.

Listening and responding

Listen with enjoyment and respond to stories, songs and other music, rhymes and poems and make up their own stories, songs, rhymes and poems.

Extend their vocabulary, exploring the meanings and sounds of new words.

Word recognition: decoding and encoding

Explore and experiment with sounds words and texts.

Understanding and interpreting texts

Extend their vocabulary exploring the meanings and sounds of new words.

Engaging with and responding to texts

Listen with enjoyment to rhymes and poems, sustain attentive listening and respond with relevant comments, questions or actions.

Related poems

'Don't Call Alligator Long Mouth Till You Cross the River' by John Agard (1986) is an amusing and easily-learned cautionary poem. Young children are bound to enjoy the name-calling in this poem and will probably delight in making up their own names to describe an alligator and perhaps other animals. For example, 'Don't call camel smelly breath till you get off his back!'

'When There's a Fire in the Jungle' by Martin Honeysett (1998) is a short rhyming poem, which considers the use of an Elephant Brigade where trunks make useful hoses.

'Our Visit to the Zoo by Jessie Pope (2007) is a short, fun rhyming poem that could easily be learned by heart by the very young. It comes from a collection of animal poems that would all support this unit of work, particularly if, as with our class, they included a zoo visit.

CHAPTER 3

Using the senses

Using our senses can be an important technique in writing creatively. Children can be encouraged to be aware of what they can see, hear, taste and touch in order to make them observe closely and record experience convincingly in poetic form. They can be encouraged to use their senses in various ways: going for listening walks, when at a given moment children stop and listen; using 'feely bags' to guess what objects are hidden inside them, and using magnifying glasses to look closely at a collection of interesting objects. Life drawing can help children to observe really closely, so for example children can have a combined arts approach where they are investigating feathers: drawing them, painting them, pressing them into wet clay tiles and using a simple straight stitch to embroider them onto interesting textiles, so that when they come to write poems about feathers they are familiar with the life form.

First-hand experience is important in using the senses. Brian, aged seven, was taken to look at the river as part of his geography work. He stopped at the weir, where a long flat glide of water slipped over the dam wall into a raging torrent, and he wrote:

> The weir.
> Oh how I love the river,
> With salmon in it and calm,
> With trout rings and waterfalls,
> Like lions roaring.

In the following poem, Elizabeth Coatsworth uses a sensory approach to describe a thunderstorm:

Rhyme

> I like to see a thunderstorm,
> A dunderstorm,

> A blunderstorm,
> I like to see it black and slow
> Come stumbling down the hills.
>
> I like to hear a thunderstorm
> A plunderstorm,
> A wonderstorm
> Roar loudly at our little house
> And shake the window sills.

(Coatsworth, 1987)

She concentrates on what the storm may look like (black and slow) and what it sounds like (roaring loudly and shaking the windowsills). Pace is emphasised as the poem builds up to a crescendo in the second stanza: a 'plunderstorm', a 'wonderstorm', rather as if the weather is breaking. There is a subtle use of personification in the words 'come stumbling' and 'roar loudly', almost as if the storm itself is a clumsy, irate god or monster, intent on frightening those in the little house.

Young children love to invent their own words as part of their language development. I think of Harry, the two year old who loves watering the garden, waving the hose pipe around with the refrain 'splish, splosh, splash'. He is playing with words, using onomatopoeia and repetition. Coatsworth uses the same technique in words like 'dunderstorm' and hints at the avarice of the storm with 'plunderstorm'.

My experience of using this poem is that after a few moments chanting, children are engaged in the catchy rhythm and begin to experiment using clenched fists to drum on the table, feet to stamp in unison and the delicate pitter-patter of fingertips to imitate raindrops heralding the storm. This body percussion can be extended to the use of musical instruments.

Paving the way

It is likely that the children will have some prior knowledge of using their senses, possibly from work related to the science curriculum. However, the following activities may provide a fun reminder for them. Both activities can be used in a classroom but probably work best in a larger space:

- For 'choose a sense', place five symbols around the room each representing a sense – for example, pictures of eyes, ears, hands, and so on. Shout out a word such as 'sea' or 'mud' and direct the children to choose a sense symbol to run to. Ask the children to describe tasting, seeing, touching, smelling or hearing. For example, if the adult shouts out 'sea' a child could run to the sight symbol and describe the sea as looking green and frothy, whereas a child running to the symbol for touch might simply say that the sea feels wet.

- For the game 'Would you rather', ask questions such as: 'Would you rather smell fish frying or bread baking?' or 'Would you rather taste strawberries or sausages?', indicating a particular area to run to.

- Once the children are familiar with both games invite them to think of their own ideas to ask the rest of the class. Not only will this support the children's familiarity with the five senses, but they will also begin to experience new words and phrases.

- Using a screen and a selection of unpitched musical instruments encourage children to guess which instrument you are using to make a sound. When the children are confident with this, use two instruments at the same time. Extend the activity into asking the children what the instruments sound like. For example, the Chinese woodblock could sound like a horse trotting; the shakers could sound like a rattlesnake.

- Ask the children which sounds remind them of a storm; shakers for example could be heavy rain, the clapperboard a sudden clap of thunder. Encourage children in groups to make their own 'thunderstorm'.

Meeting the poem

- Using photographic images or video clips introduce the children to the theme of thunderstorms. Encourage them to talk about their own experiences and how they feel about storms. Ask questions such as, 'Do you like being outside or inside in a thunderstorm?' Be prepared for some children's fears to be expressed and encourage empathy.

- Model telling a true story of when you were caught up in a storm and invite other adults in the room to do the same.

- Give the children time to think about their own stories and share them with each other.

- Read the poem yourself at least twice. If you have additional adults or parents working with you, let them read it too. It is important that children understand that readings may be different. Ask the children what the person in the poem appears to think about thunderstorms and why they might think this way. In this case the writer's view is positive 'I like to see a thunderstorm'. Do they agree?

- Discuss the play on the word 'thunderstorm' leading to 'blunderstorm', 'plunderstorm' and 'wonderstorm', making sure that the children understand 'blunder', 'plunder' and 'wonder'.

Presenting and performing

- Try a shared reading of the poem using an enlarged image. By dividing the class in half and allocating a verse to each group you will enable the children to both speak and hear the poem.

- Introduce the idea of using sound effects for accompaniment. Demonstrate how children can recreate the sound of raindrops by using their fingers to drum on their knees, at first gently and then with increasing force. This might mean building up the number of children doing this until the whole class is involved.

- Provide small groups with a number of percussion instruments and materials for creating sounds. Cardboard 'wobbled' makes good thunder. Encourage the groups to create a **soundscape** for the poem. It is important to

I like to see a thunderstorm

A dunderstorm

A blunderstorm

I like to see it, black and slow

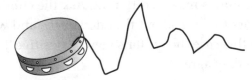

Come stumbling down the hills

Figure 3.1 Musical score for unpitched instruments.

practise percussion so that the voices are complemented and not drowned out with an over-enthusiastic 'board wobbler'. When the group is satisfied with their sound accompaniments a laminated copy of the poem can be 'scored'.

- Perform with the whole class, or each group could perform their interpretation to other groups. In this way children experience different interpretations and are given an opportunity to make comments in relation to their peers' presentations.

- The way in which one reads this poem can be changed simply by substituting the word 'like' with an antonym such as 'hate'. The class may wish to try saying the poem with this small alteration and consider the difference that one word makes to their performance.

Reading, writing and reflecting

- Write in the first person as someone who has been caught in a thunderstorm, relating this to the oral storytelling described in 'paving the way'. This could be done in various ways, through shared and guided writing, storyboarding or the teacher scribing children's dramatic accounts.

- Reflect upon the inferred personification included in the poem by asking the children: 'What do the words "roar" and "stumbling" make you think of?', 'Which creatures might do this?' and 'If we said the poem is like an animal, which animal might it be – a dragon or a lion or a huge bear?' Ask the children to close their eyes and imagine what physical shape the storm might take. Children can then use **visualisation** to draw the storm in animal form.

- Set up a role play area where children can play at being the weather forecaster, surrounded by maps and visual images.

- Word banks can be set up in various ways; for example, a 'spidergram' could record ways of describing rain, thunder and lightning:

torrential

⇑

light ⇐ rain ⇒ heavy

⇓

pouring

Alternatively, children could paint pictures of a thunderstorm and the words could be mounted on these.

Becoming a poet

- Scaffold children's writing by providing a skeleton verse and asking them to help you complete it. For example:

> I like to feel a rainyshower,
> a _____ , a _____
> I like to feel it w_____ and _____
> Come _____ down my face.

could become:

> I like to feel a rainyshower,
> a drainyshower, a painyshower
> I like to feel it wet and wild
> Come pouring down my face.

- Use other related works in the same way. For example, in 'Sounds' by Irene Rawsley (2000), the poet's lines:

> The spookiest sound in the world must be
> A ghost singing sounds in a hollow tree

could become:

> The spookiest sound in the world must be
> A witch putting nasty spells on me

In using 'Morning' by Grace Nichols (2005), the poet's lines:

> Morning comes
>   with a milk float jiggling
> Morning comes
>   with a milkman whistling

could become:

> Night time comes
>   with baby crying
> Night time comes
>   with daddy snoring

How it worked in the classroom

The children, a mixture from Year 1 and reception classes, were keen to invent words for the games and liked the idea of moving around and having to think quickly. The teacher used a game in which each child was either the sun, a house, rain or a storm. Children sat in a circle and the teacher created a narrative from the poem:

> Once upon a time there were some very, very small children and they lived in a house on the hill. One night there was the gentle whispering of rain. It grew louder and louder and finally a storm broke . . .

When the children heard 'their' word they swapped places. The teacher thought that this would sustain attentive listening and get them used to working together. She was also aware that narrative is a more familiar form to children. Two teachers then took it in turns to read the poem, giving it their own particular style of delivery. They commented on each other's readings, modelling response 'Mr Moore I could hear thunder in your voice', to encourage the children to be critical. The poem was mounted against a backdrop of a storm on the IWB.

The teachers had made paper images of lightning, rain drops and thunder clouds on which the children stuck descriptive words, written on Post-it® notes. Words for rain included 'depressing', 'hard' and 'very scary'. The teachers gave each child an instrument or helped them with body percussion such as rubbing their hands together, slapping their legs or clicking their fingers, and the children were able to follow the score on the IWB. There were several performances and the final one was recorded on an MP3 player for the children to listen to.

Plate 3.1 Following the score on the interactive whiteboard.

At a later ICT session the children were encouraged to make up their own storm pictures.

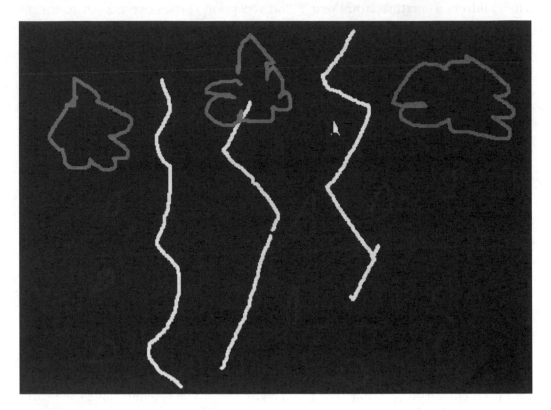

Figure 3.2 Harry, aged 6, used dramatic colours, lightning and clouds to portray the drama of a storm.

Related objectives to the Primary Framework for Literacy Foundation Stage and Year 1

Speaking

Enjoy listening to and using spoken and written language and readily turn to it in play and learning.

Extend their vocabulary, exploring the meanings and sounds of new words.

Interpret a text by reading aloud with some variety in pace and emphasis.

Listening and responding

Listen with enjoyment and respond to rhymes and poems and make up their own rhymes and poems.

Listen with sustained concentration, building new stores of words.

Understanding and interpreting texts

Know that print carries meaning and in English is read from left to right and top to bottom.

Engaging with and responding to texts

Listen with enjoyment to rhymes and poems, sustain attentive listening and respond.

Visualise and comment on events, characters and ideas, making imaginative links to own experience.

Creating and shaping texts

Find and use new and interesting words and phrases.

Related poems

'Sounds' by Irene Rawsley (2000) invites the reader to consider what might be the noisiest, tiniest, spookiest or happiest sound. This should provide lively discussion and support children's writing.

'The Sound Collector' by Roger McGough (2003) explores the notion of collecting sounds, putting them all in a bag and taking them away. Children might like to table which sounds they would miss alongside ones they wouldn't.

'This is the Hand' by Michael Rosen (1981) has a similar rhythmic pattern to 'The House that Jack Built', so works well when you add actions.

'I Like to Stay Up' by Grace Nichols (2005) is all about listening to ghost stories and then wishing you hadn't.

'I Love' by Marc Matthews (1994) describes the evocative smell of home-baked bread and cakes.

CHAPTER 4

Pattern and rhyme

Patterned texts form an important part of young children's reading repertoires as they are easy to learn, ingratiating themselves into their memories so that they are always to hand for children to relive and enjoy. They are also important for reading development as they encourage prediction in reading, inviting children to make well-informed guesses as to the next word. It is not only repeated words and phrases that help young readers; rhyme and rhythm can also help us to anticipate words and decode those that are unfamiliar.

Tony Mitton writes engagingly for young readers. His poems are often alliterative and patterned but demand more of the reader than simple chanting.

The Bag

Nobody comes to the gate.
Because of the bag.

Nobody knocks on the door.
Because of the bag.

Nobody enters the house.
Because of the bag.

Nobody sits in the room.
Because of the bag.

Nobody kindles the fire.
Because of the bag.

Because of the bag.

The bag in the hearth.

The bag in the hearth
with thorns and bones.

The bag with beads
and burrs and stones.

The bag with rue
and a sprig of thyme:

a strange collection
of things to rhyme,

of things to finger
and things to tell,

and things to cast
their silent spell.

And nobody comes to the house.
Because of the bag.

(Tony Mitton, 1998)

I was drawn to this poem from the first reading for a variety of reasons. First, the poem develops an air of mystery about something as commonplace as a bag. Second, its rhythmic pattern, changing as it does halfway through the poem, heightens the reader's anticipation and begs to be read aloud. The simple chorus '*Because of the bag*' in the first half entices us into the poem and we're not expecting the rich mix of more unusual words such as 'burrs' and 'thyme', which follow in the second half. I am intrigued by the juxtaposition of the objects in the bag. Why 'thorns and bones'? Why 'burrs and stones'? In what other context would they come together, other than in a spell or voodoo? Initially I thought this was too ambitious a poem for Year 1 children to enjoy. I was wrong.

There are many possibilities for approaching this work. It arouses an innate curiosity about people and their possessions. What do the things we carry around with us reveal ? What is it that makes certain belongings important to us and not others? What would we find in the plastic carrier of a tramp or a Gucci bag from a top model? The bag in the poem is clearly important. We understand from the first two lines, 'Nobody comes to the house / *Because of the bag*', that it is menacing. We discover the contents but there are still important questions unanswered. Who does this bag belong to? Why is it sitting sentinel in the hearth, dissuading all comers? Who owns it? Who decided what would go in it and why? These questions can be explored in the following suggested sequence.

Paving the way

- Seat the children in a circle placing an empty bag in the middle. The bag should be interesting to fire children's imaginations; for example, a battered evening bag from a charity shop, a sack tied with string on which some sea shells have been threaded or a bag made from unusual material. You might want to give an explanation for having the bag, for example, that you found it in your house when you moved in and you don't know why it was left there. Any plausible explanation will suffice as long as there is an air of mystery surrounding it.

- Give the children time to think. Model the questions that the bag poses to you: Who has owned the bag? Is it an old person, a young person, a real person? What might be inside it? Why was it left where you found it? The children do not necessarily need to answer these questions; they are simply scaffolds for thinking.

- Model how to take something imaginary from the bag then describe it to the class. Give the children time to think about what might also be inside the bag then ask them to **mime** taking something and describe it to the others in small groups.

- An alternative to this activity is to **mime** using an object from the bag, for example a hand mirror, and encourage the children to guess what it is. Accept all ideas, however simple.

Meeting the poem

- Before the lesson, familiarise yourself with the poem. You may like to practise reading this out loud to yourself in various ways for best effect, being aware of how the rhythm changes halfway through.

- Read the poem to the children at least twice without showing them the text, then re-read it using an IWB or enlarged copy to show the writing. Although not all children will be able to read all the words, you can demonstrate important reading concepts such as directionality and word correspondence. Children need to see poems to understand that they are written differently to prose; in this case, a long narrow poem leads the reader rather like a pathway leading to the house in the text.

- Encourage the children to practise together saying the line '*Because of the bag*'. You may like to practise this in different ways, stressing different words, for example '*Because* of the bag', 'Because of *the bag*'. Highlighting this on the written text will support the children while you read the other lines. This scaffolds children's reading so that everyone can join in.

- Ask them to listen to the poem and look closely at the way it is written. Encourage the children to consider where and when the pattern changes. This can be highlighted on the IWB.

- The words within the poem may introduce some children to new vocabulary such as 'sprig', 'rue', 'burr' and 'hearth'. This may be a good time to explore these by discussing meanings, showing pictures or making a collection of the contents of the bag.

- Tell the children to imagine visiting the house described in the poem; however, explain that the house has been locked up recently and barbed wire encircles it. This restriction means that they will only be able to imagine looking through the windows and seeing the inside of the house. This helps children to focus deeply on an imaginative response and controls movement in a way that simply allowing the children to wander through 'the house' might not.

- Explain the drama to the children:

  We're going to walk around the house, look in through the windows and see what we can see, being very quiet as we don't know who might be here and whether or not we should be around. Remember what you can see, hear and smell.

- Encourage the children to talk to you and each other while they explore the house, but in whispered tones to preserve the tension.

- Gather the children together and discuss what they saw, felt, smelt and heard. Try to incorporate all of their ideas. If, for example, a child volunteers that they have seen a picture of a person, discuss: who was it of? What did they look like? Where was it hanging? Did anyone else see it?

- Explain to the children that they might find out more about the bag and owner by getting a closer look inside the house; however, suggest it is safer if only two people do this rather than the whole class, who might more easily disturb whoever is inside. Ask two children to go back to the house and see if they can find a gap in the fence. Involve the other children who are sitting around the fence by first asking them if they can see any ways in through the barbed wire. The class is likely to have many suggestions, which can be considered and the most effective used; for example, you might use a low hole in the hedge to enter but a rusty gate that they could run through for a quick exit. This concentration on detail strengthens their belief in the drama.

- Warn the children that someone has been seen in the garden recently and to be prepared to meet them. Introduce some rules for the two intruders. Encourage the remainder of the class to think of these: 'Remember not to damage anything. You are in someone's property. Be polite to anyone you might meet but don't do anything you don't want to. Stay together.'

- Encourage the class to sit quietly as they watch the two trespassers miming their entrance and exploration. While the children are doing this, prepare yourself for **teacher in role**. You may perhaps use a simple prop such as a headscarf. As **teacher in role** meet the children and ask them what they are doing. You could introduce yourself as a neighbour and start by being quite cross at the intrusion.

- Maintaining your role, gather all the children together and let them ask you questions about the house, its owner and the bag (**hot seating**). It is important to remember that the poem is central to this drama, so be prepared in your story to refer to it. For example, you might say:

  > I've been a neighbour for many years and I remember the day that Mrs/Mr Twitch came to the house. She's never been too friendly and people say she's strange. You never see her without her bag. Sometimes at night she wanders around with it on her shoulder. What do you think she does with it?

- Using **improvisation**, ask each child to adopt the role of the owner of the bag, while they wander around the garden collecting things. Remind them of their movements and facial expressions. They may, for example, mime picking up things to put into their bag. From time to time, freeze the action and ask some of the children to say in role what they are thinking and doing (**thought tracking**).

- Explore the contents of the bag or the house by means of **physical theatre** (sometimes described as **white drama**). Ask the children individually to take on the shape of something in the bag or the house. Start by giving the children suggestions before you progress to asking them for their ideas. For example, you might ask individuals to freeze as a bone, a spider or a spikey burr. Work towards groups collaborating, for example, as the gate in the poem or fire in the hearth. The **freeze frame** could then come to life as in the gate opening or the fire flickering. This work could then be incorporated into the children's performance of the poem.

Presenting and performing

- Provide the groups with copies of the poem and suggest that they discuss how they might present it for an audience.

- Allow the groups plenty of time to learn the poem off by heart and practise and revise their performances before they share these with others. Children could work on this at separate times in guided activities, supported by an adult.

- Following performances, encourage each group to explain why and how they chose to present as they did and give time for their audience to respond. If children are not familiar with doing this you may need to model being a critical friend: 'I really liked the way you used your voice, it made me shiver. Next time you perform the poem perhaps you could add some action to stress your point even more.'

Plate 4.1 Performing the poem.

Reading, writing and reflecting

- Ask the children to imagine and draw what the owner of the bag looks like. Additionally they could produce a cross section of the bag in order to reveal its contents, perhaps adding words or phrases to it. The bag could contain contents from the original poem or include new items arising from the children's improvisation.

- Focus on the lines 'a strange collection / of things to rhyme': search the poem for the contents of the bag that rhyme. Model writing them together, for example, 'bones and stones'.

- Invite the children, either independently or in pairs, to make a list of other rhyming things which might be in the bag. Remember to suggest that they say the words out loud to avoid pairings such as 'blood and food' in favour of words such as 'blood and mud'. This will contextualise and strengthen children's phonological awareness and understanding of phonics. You may want to support this activity by providing a list of words as starting points.

Becoming a poet

- Model writing a poem in shared or guided work with the whole class or a group using the format of 'The Bag' or one of the other related poems.

- Share the related poems with the class. The following activities can scaffold writing. 'Ten Things Found in a Wizard's Pocket' by Ian McMillan could be rewritten as ten things found in a king's pocket, an alien's pocket, and so on. The traditional tale 'In a Dark, Dark House' could be changed to another setting, such as a dark, dark ship. Similarly the first few lines of 'The Bag', which do not rhyme but maintain a rhythm, could be changed, for example:

> Nobody comes to the moat.
> *Because of the bag*

> Nobody comes to the drawbridge.
> Because of the bag

The chorus '*Because of the bag*' could become 'Because of the sack', 'the box', 'the bottle'. Possibilities are endless. When the poems are written the children could devise presentations of these and perform alongside the original.

How it worked in the classroom

The teacher who we initially approached to work with us on this poem had reservations about using it as she was uncomfortable with the vocabulary used. It is important that you use a poem with which you feel a rapport; otherwise, you cannot demonstrate the engagement you are trying to inculcate in the children. Given the wide choice of poetry available it is worth searching for those with which you can work enthusiastically.

Plate 4.2 Teacher in role.

Interestingly, a teacher who taught a parallel Year 1 class immediately engaged with the poem and welcomed the opportunity to work with it. Having played some of the games suggested in 'paving the way', she read the poem and then used the written version displayed on an IWB. She considered it important to help children's understanding of the unfamiliar vocabulary in the poem by using internet images of a hearth and real examples of bones, burrs and herbs, which the class were able to handle. When it came to the **improvisation**, she marked out the floor area of the 'house' by using plastic PE cones. This clearly defined the drama area and resulted in children confidently using their working space. **Improvisation** was initiated and concluded by the use of a signal familiar to the class, in this case a sharp clap. When the teacher took the role of a neighbour she wore a hat, carried a stick and adopted a stooping gait. She used a walking stick to point to individual children. This strategy supported children's belief in her as the neighbour, and helped in the management of choosing which child might ask the next question without using names. The teacher initially adopted a **high status role**. She used a commanding voice alongside a rather grumpy approach to the 'intruders'. As the children began to ask questions, her **teacher in role** status moved from **middle** to **low** as she began to ask for the children's ideas and help. Consequently the initial tension while the teacher was in tight control gradually

Figure 4.1
Luca, aged 5, has drawn a picture of the owner of the bag.

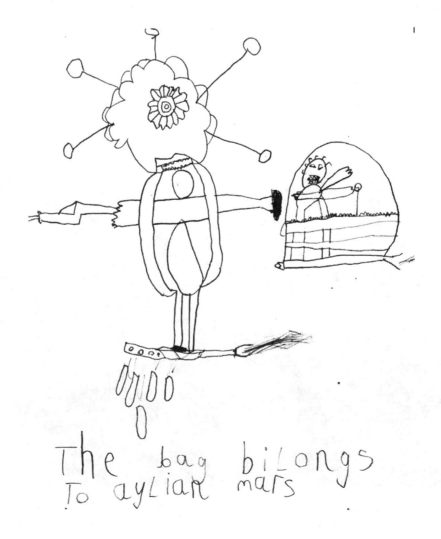

The bag bilongs To ayliak mars

Figure 4.2
Harry, aged 5, has drawn a picture of the vampire who he thinks owns the bag.

Pattern and rhyme

relaxed as the children entered into the drama more deeply and the teacher was able to hand over more of the discussion to them.

When the teacher initiated a poetry performance, she divided her class and the poem into two and invited each group to prepare their parts. Both groups had an adult to support them and mediate if necessary. Although the teaching focus was on recitation the children, without direction, emphasised the phrase '*because of the bag*' by stepping forward and pointing. Later in their work the class were invited to describe in **multi-modal texts** who might own the bag.

The following examples of children's written work show important evidence of **intertextuality**.

Luca includes details of extra terrestrial creatures from fantasy texts. It is interesting that he has chosen to depict an 'aylian' as the poem suggests that the owner of the bag is alienated from society. Whereas Harry (Figure 4.2) depicts the owner as a vampire with companions, perhaps an echo of the familiars associated with witches.

Both pieces of work are evidence of children's imaginative, personal and confident response to a text challenging for young language users.

Related outcomes from the Primary Framework for Literacy Year 1

Speaking

Interpret a text by reading aloud with some variety in pace and emphasis.

Listening and responding

Listen with sustained concentration, building new stores of words in different contexts.

Group discussion and interaction

Ask and answer relevant questions, make relevant contributions, offer suggestions and take turns.

Drama

Explore familiar themes and characters through improvisation and role play.

Word recognition

Read more challenging texts, which can be decoded using acquired phonic knowledge and skills along with automatic recognition of high frequency words.

Understanding and interpreting texts

Explore the effect of patterns of language and repeated words and phrases.

Engaging with and responding to texts

Visualise and comment on events, characters and ideas, making imaginative links to own experiences.

Creating and shaping texts

Find new and interesting words and phrases including story language.

Text structure and organisation

Write chronological and non-chronological texts using simple structures.

Related poems

A Dark, Dark Tale by Ruth Brown (1981) is a picture book derived from the traditional rhyme 'In a Dark, Dark House.' This book's beautiful illustrations, depicting the mysterious and moody interior of an old mansion might support the drama work very well. The front cover portrays a cat who becomes our feline guide as we wander deeper and deeper into the seemingly abandoned house, but whose house is it, and what will the reader find at the end of their journey? The pattern of this tale lends itself to further adapted rhymes as previously suggested.

'Ten Things You Find in a Wizard's Pocket' by Ian Macmillan (2000) provides us with a list of contents, not all of which are quite what you might expect. This is another poem that could scaffold children's writing of list poems.

'The Magic Box' by Kit Wright (1987) is a poem that describes the contents of a box. The contents are magical exciting the imagination of the reader and inviting us to play with new ideas and possibilities. Importantly, this is a beautifully written poem and lends itself to being performed with ritual.

CHAPTER 5

Poems on a theme

Themes are important in children's learning. As humans we try to make sense of the world around us and schema theory suggests that we tend to store much of what we know in schemata, which are simply memory 'containers' for our experiences. We could, for example, have a poetry schema where we store all we know about poetry. This, however, is insufficient to help us to read and understand poetry, as we need to make connections between what we know and what we are struggling to understand. In order to fully make sense of a poem about the snow, for example, we need memories of it falling, drifting, melting, freezing and riming the hedgerows. As we need to bring so much of our wider world knowledge to reading and writing it can be powerful to organise children's learning in themes or topics – a common practice in the 1980s and 1990s, and one that has been revived by the publication *Excellence and Enjoyment* (DfES, 2003). This encourages schools to take control of their curriculum and be flexible in their organisation and the Qualification and Assessment Authority (QCA) has encouraged teachers to take a cross-curricular approach to their work through the QCA/DfES-published schemes of work.

For this chapter, we could have chosen many themes that link with the wider curriculum. We chose dragons because we don't seem to be able to do without them. They feature in diverse cultures, usually as resplendent scaly creatures armed with fierce claws and fiery breath. Western cultures tend to regard them as wicked and malevolent but in China they are revered as being kind and clever. Poems about dragons are particularly suitable for themed work as it is easy to link them to other poems and stories. Children love to draw and design two- and three-dimensional dragons, while dance sessions offer the opportunity for children to move together as one huge creature. Some cultures believe that dragons can only be seen by those who truly believe in them – a sentiment held about fairies in J. M. Barrie's *Peter Pan*. Belief in dragons is cleverly described in the following poem:

Dragon

Look very lightly
look that way –
I saw a dragon there
yesterday;

His ears were open,
his eyes were shut
his scales were as hard
as a coconut.

His body was thick,
his tail was strong,
it stretched round the railings
ten feet long . . .

His snores were thunderous,
dark and deep,
He breathed like an engine
in his sleep.

Look through your lashes
faint and small . . .
can you see anyone
there at all,

Down by the railings,
way-away?
I saw a dragon there
yesterday.

(Kenward, 1998)

This poem is challenging as we're not quite sure whether to believe the poet or not. She speaks to us in a conspiratorial tone as if sharing a secret. We suspect that she actually touched the dragon as she seems sure his scales were as 'hard as a coconut', but we're not sure whether he was asleep or not as 'his ears were open [but] his eyes were shut'. There is a clever use of rhyme, which makes the poem easy to memorise, and we are able to picture and 'hear' the dragon because of detail such as 'thick tail' and 'thunderous snores'. The poet addresses us directly and assumes that we are young: 'Look through your lashes faint and small', and hints at danger by advising: 'Look very lightly'. Warned like this, would we dare to stare?

Children's prior experience of dragons is likely to be culturally grounded. Some children may think of the dragon dancing at Chinese New Year celebrations; others may recall having seen a dragon depicted in a story book or on a flag or a coat of arms. However, other children will have little or no experience and paving the way is especially important for them.

Paving the way

- Use a three-dimensional dragon, for example, a stuffed toy or hand puppet, and put this in a cloth bag. Introduce a story: 'There is a little creature in my bag who has spent the whole night in the classroom, can you guess what it is?' Allow children to feel the model and give out clues: 'It has very scaly skin and sharp claws, it breathes fire and it's got a very long tail with a sharp point.' Reveal the dragon and compare it with other images.

- Ask the children to close their eyes and think of their own dragon. Talk them through the **visualisation** by using simple questions such as: 'Is your dragon big or small, fat or thin, long or short?'

- Devise a word bank of descriptive words about dragons. This may work better as a small group activity, which can be repeated until the whole class has taken part.

- Having collected describing words for their dragon's appearance repeat the process with words to describe the personality of the dragon: fierce or timid, quiet or noisy, safe or dangerous.

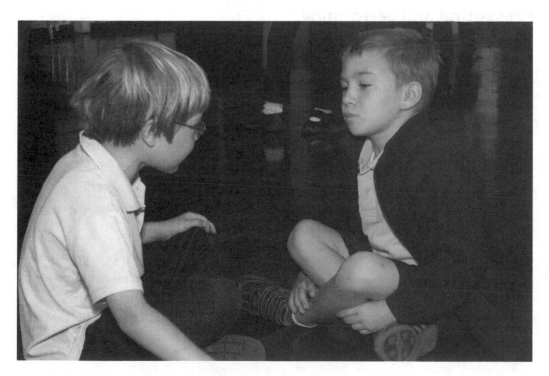

Plate 5.1 Gossip partners.

Meeting the poem

There is the opportunity here to use two drama techniques: **teacher in role** and gossip partners.

- As **teacher in role**, introduce the poem as a true story in a conspiratorial tone. This will be more convincing if you memorise it first.

- Organise gossip partners. Put the children into pairs A or B. Ask child A to be the 'I' of the poem; in other words, the one who has seen the dragon. Invite child B to ask child A about the time when he/she saw the dragon. Providing child B with an opening line helps to get the 'gossip' flowing; for example, 'Did you really see a dragon?' The pair can then swap roles so that both children will have had an opportunity to describe the event and ask questions.

- Invite willing pairs to perform their improvised conversation to the class. By watching more than one **improvisation** children should be able to appreciate how interpretations differ.

- Invite groups of children to build a dragon with their bodies (**physical theatre**). Support them in considering how to represent the tail, ears and so on. This could be shared with others as a **freeze frame** or children could move together as the dragon. You could use a piece of music or simply beat a tambourine to encourage rhythmic movement.

Presenting and performing

- Using an IWB or other means show the written version of the poem and share a reading. Check that the children understand all the vocabulary.

- Split your class into two groups: the story tellers and the describers. One half of the class performs verses 1, 5 and 6 whilst the other half verses 2, 3, and 4. The two parts will need very different voices; for example, persuasive in verses 1, 5 and 6 but sceptical in the other verses. The line 'He breathed like a dragon in his sleep' can be expressed sceptically as a question rather than a statement.

- Alternatively, divide the class into groups of six. Each child takes one verse and memorises it. They then practise each verse in sequence. In the final performance, pupils freeze in a particular pose; for example, the storyteller might be holding up their forefinger to the audience. Then each child comes out of the freeze frame to recite and in turn listen to the next performer.

Reading, writing and reflecting

● Start a collection of dragon images. The children can add to these either by using search engines or by bringing images or artefacts from home. Talk about these with the children and make a class display. Discuss favourites.

● Children may enjoy painting dragons and using collage to represent 'scales as hard as a coconut'. Printing a dragon can be very successful; simple potato prints overlap convincingly to make scales.

● As part of shared or guided writing you may wish to invent a newspaper headline to fit the sighting of the dragon. By providing an initial example children can often invent their own; for example, 'Dragon seen roaring round railings', 'Dragon's scales scare shoppers' or 'Dragon flies into town breathing fire'. Once you have your headline you can either use the children's ideas to scribe a report of the sighting or pre-write a report for the children to edit with you acting as scribe.

At some point in this unit of work you may encounter a child or children who think(s) deeply about the poem and suggests that the 'dragon' may have been something else. If this does not happen you may want to appear sceptical by posing questions such as: 'Did the poet really see a dragon? Could it have been something that looked and sounded like a dragon?' Reading the poem with particular stress on line three may make children start to wonder: 'He breathed like an engine / in his sleep.' An interesting discussion may emerge. If the children suggest the dragon might be a train or digger you could return to the **physical theatre** activity described in 'meeting the poem'. The children could show their mechanical dragons (trains, road sweepers, gritting lorries) through **freeze frames** or moving representations. Sound effects from the children or from percussion instruments could support.

Becoming a poet

● Starting with their images of dragons and using the word banks gathered in 'paving the way', support the children in writing their own dragon poems. This could be based on an appeal to find a lost dragon and supported by a writing frame:

> **Lost**
> One dragon
>
> _____ _____
>
> _____ _____
>
> *Last seen:*
>
> _____ _____

● Here are two examples that you could model writing to the children:

Lost	Lost
One dragon	One dragon
sharp claws,	green scales,
fiery breath,	hot breath,
pointed tail,	sly smile,
Last seen:	*Last seen:*
strolling in the park	lighting a bonfire

● Alternatively, the children could compose **acrostic** poems.

How it worked in the classroom

When we visited the school, the classroom was already festooned with dragons. Children had brought in puppets and models from home and the teacher had found some exciting images and dragon music on the internet. The children had worked together on an irate hand-printed dragon; on each of the creatures' spiny scales, a word described the bad-tempered beast. Beside the dragon was a list where children had simply composed a line such as 'you snort fire' and 'you eat cinders'.

Plate 5.2 An irate dragon made of hand prints.

The children had clearly acquired a rich vocabulary to describe the mythical beasts and the teacher had thought carefully about introducing the drama. She kept a dragon in her desk drawer and bought it out dramatically, encouraging children to ask it questions such as 'Have you been here all night?' The dragon answered by 'whispering' to the teacher. In order to visualise their own dragon, the teacher gave each child an imaginary photo frame, which they held in their open palm while they described their dragon to others. This helped to focus them on the task.

As an introductory drama activity the teacher asked children to line up as railings, which might have been unfamiliar . A pupil **in role** as the dragon then breathed and curled his way through the railings, and the children 'looked through their lashes' before the teacher, in role as a bystander, gave a recount of what she'd seen. The children then went straight into their gossip partners.

They all gave accounts of what they had seen and then worked as groups to move together as a dragon. This involved a lot of thought about what the dragon looked like, what part of his body each child should be and how he should move. The children cooperated to synchronise movement so that the group moved convincingly as one creature.

Back in the classroom, the poetry performance work was supported by simple changes; as multiple voices were used, the 'I' in the poem became 'we'. The children held up their fingers for 'ten feet long', snored rhythmically to introduce verse four and beat their chests to the line 'his scales were as hard as a coconut'. Multiple voices are supportive in encouraging children to speak aloud with confidence.

In making the newspaper headlines, the teacher used shared writing. By making a sentence frame on the IWB and dragging words onto it, the children were able to compose various headlines and discuss which were most effective.

The poetry writing was guided. The teacher worked with groups modelling and demonstrating how to write an **acrostic** poem. Callum (aged five) wrote:

> Down in a swamp
> Rests a dragon
> And bones of people
> Getting older and
> Older
> Nearly white sand.

This is a sophisticated poem, which indicates that he has thought carefully about the habitat ('a swamp') and has chosen words carefully; the dragon 'rests'. Perhaps his most sophisticated use of language is the metaphor for bones, 'nearly white

Plate 5.3 Physical theatre: becoming a dragon.

sand', which gives a dreamy, timeless feel to the poem, reminding us that dragons are old, very old.

Writing was extended into story form. Eleanor (aged five) wrote:

> Once upon a time there was a girl. She decided to go and see her granny. so she got on her bike and set off. When she got to her granny she was not there but there was a dragon. The dragon swallowed. The girl managed to open the dragon's mouth. And replaced it with a gingerbread man. The girl ran home without stopping. Her mum were very glad to see her and they lived happily ever after. (Spelling has been corrected.)

There is strong evidence of **intertextuality** in this writing. Eleanor relies upon a story schema, which includes Red Riding Hood and the Gingerbread Man, and confidently uses story language such as 'once upon a time' and 'they lived happily ever after'. Eleanor knows that 'once upon a time' is an invitation to suspend disbelief. In her story, little girls are allowed to roam freely without adult supervision and are brave enough to prise open the jaws of a dragon. She is connecting what she has learned of dragons with what she already knows in order to extend her rich knowledge and understanding of children's literature. She might also be drawing from *Shrek*, a series of animated postmodern films, which include characters from traditional tales. She has the confidence to update her story; the girl goes to see her granny 'on a bike'. Her ideas are the driving force behind Eleanor's writing, as her teacher has given her a rich mixture of poetry and drama to encourage her ideas to flow.

Related objectives from the Primary Framework for Literacy for Year 1

Speaking

Retell stories ordering events using story language.

Experiment with and build new stores of words to communicate in different contexts.

Listening and responding

Listen with sustained concentration, building new stores of words in different contexts.

Group discussion and interaction

Take turns to speak, listen to others' suggestions and talk about what they are going to do.

Drama

Explore familiar themes and characters through improvisation and role play.

Word recognition

Read more challenging texts, which can be decoded using their acquired phonic knowledge and skills along with automatic recognition of high-frequency words.

Word structure and spelling

Spell new words using phonics as the prime approach.

Understanding and interpreting texts

Make predictions showing an understanding of ideas, events and characters.

Engaging with and responding to text

Visualise and comment on events, characters and ideas, making imaginative links to their own experiences.

Creating and shaping texts

Find and use new and interesting words and phrases, including story language.

Related poems

'The Toaster' by William Jay Smith (2001) is a poem that poses the question: 'Is this about a dragon or a kitchen appliance?' Let your class decide.

'The Dragon in the Cellar' by Nick Toczek (1997) is a humorous and very rhythmic poem. Being quite lengthy, it might represent a challenge for young children to learn off by heart; however, it has a catchy and easily-learned chorus. The dragon in the cellar is joined by other dragons such as the dragon in the loo and the dragon in the study, but are they quite what they appear to be? This poem could stimulate some interesting discussions and make an action-packed performance.

'A Small Dragon' by Brian Patten (2001) is a favourite poem of ours as we have both used it successfully with young children despite it having been written originally for adults. It describes a dragon found in a woodshed and poses some important questions about belief and responsibility. Its rather more serious subject matter could prove an interesting read alongside more humorous dragon poems. You can find a recording of the poet reading this poem at www.poetryarchive.org/ children'sarchive.

For poems about every kind of dragon, try the illustrated *Dragon Poems* (Foster, 2004).

Patterns on the page

Children of the twenty-first century inhabit a world where they are surrounded by texts; some in print and some screen-based. This means that children are familiar with multimodality: texts that combine words and pictures, movement and sound. Teachers need to recognise this and support children in engaging with multimodality, both as readers and writers. Using shape poems, sometimes called **concrete poems**, is an exciting way to do this. **Concrete poems** are designed graphically to position poetry in dramatic ways on the white space of the page. In reading these poems we cannot ignore the graphic form; it is an important dimension of what the writer is trying to say.

There is an infinite variety of **concrete poems**. James Carter, an innovative new voice in poetry, uses pattern in sonic and graphic form. His poem 'Vacuum Cleaner', for example, is cleverly written in the shape of a full-sized machine including handle, bag, motor and carpet, with a flex leading us away to . . . who, we wonder (see Figure 6.1 on p. 52).

The form of the poem affects the way in which we read it. We read the words 'just plug me in and turn me on' slowly as our eye scans down the white space, before we are able to gather speed as the lines become longer: 'pull my lead out nice and long – push me round the carpet floors and . . .'. The graphics, which make up the rim of the machine and the carpet using exclamation marks and upper-case 'M's, are an invitation to make up our own sound effects.

John Hegley is another poet who experiments extravagantly with the white space of the page. He uses shape, form, colour, size, and integral images in order to emphasise the aesthetic qualities of the poem. The untitled poem in Figure 6.2 is written around an image of a hand, held up as if in supplication. The words can only be read easily if we turn the page around, and this slow pace adds to the quality of atonement. A moment is captured in our minds of the honest hand being crumpled into an aggressive fist that commits an act of unsolicited violence in the incongruous context of children making sand castles. Although both utilise shape imaginatively, the two poems are very different: one is a catchy, rhythmic

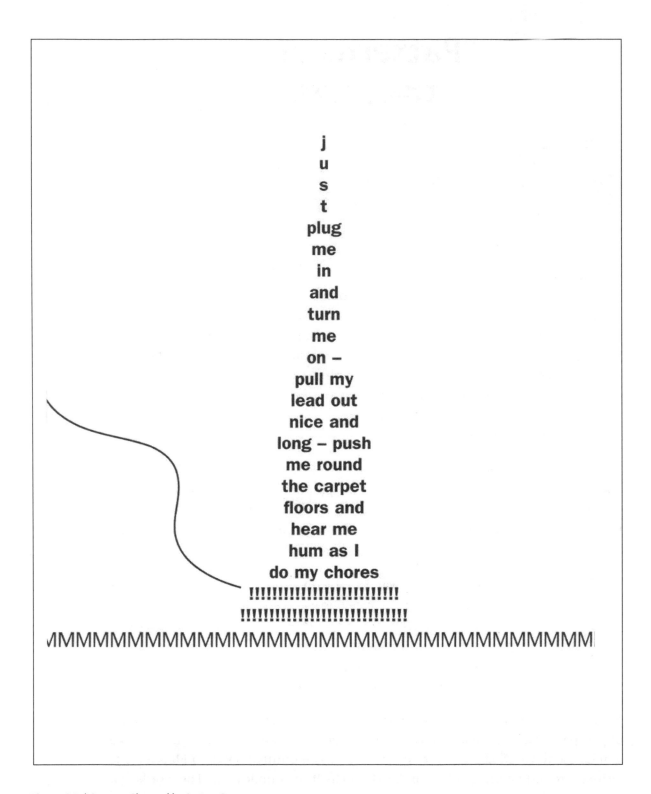

Figure 6.1 'Vacuum Cleaner' by James Carter.

Source: From J. Carter (2001), *Cars Stars Electric Guitars*, reproduced by permission of Walker Books Ltd, London SE11 5HJ.

Figure 6.2 'Untitled' by John Hegley (2002).

Source: Reprinted by permission of PFD on behalf of John Hegley © 2002.

verse easy to commit to memory and entertaining; the other, a thought-provoking confession that makes us reflect on human behaviour. Hegley's poem is an exciting example of **free verse**: there are rhyming words ('hand' and 'land'), but these are not found at the ends of lines, which is a more common linguistic feature of poetry.

Reading works such as these encourages children to push their own boundaries as writers. They can use an exciting range of pencils, crayons and other mark-making media and improve their use of ICT and ability to compose texts on-screen by playing with features such as alignment, line spacing, use of imported images, font and colour.

Here is a teaching sequence for 'Untitled'.

Paving the way

- Show the children the poem, preferably in an enlarged form so that you can annotate. When using **concrete poems** it is important to show children the poem as a first encounter, as the poet has designed his work for immediate visual impact.

- Ask the children to identify the image and connect with instances where people might hold up their open palm to others. Children may think of traffic police or Native American greetings.

Meeting the poem

- Read aloud pointing to the words. Pause and let the children reflect for a moment. Memorise the poem yourself and, holding up your own hand to the children, repeat without reading.

- Explain to the children that you are in role and ask, 'How do you think I feel?' Make your hand into an angry fist as you **mime** smashing the sandcastle and change your expression to match. Encourage the children to make 'angry fists' and open 'sorry hands' and change their expressions accordingly.

Presenting and performing

- Encourage children to memorise and recite the poem to each other with appropriate expression and intonation. Encourage children to experiment; they might, for example, say the poem in a reluctant kind of way, as it they had been forced to apologise.

Reading, writing and reviewing

- Model telling a story from your own life when you were really sorry and then encourage the children to share their stories with each other.

- Using performance space, allow time for a drama session beginning with some **visualisation**. Ask children to lie down and listen to the music of the sea. Encourage them to imagine a sandy beach with the sea gently lapping on the shore and a warm breeze playing. Direct them to sit up slowly and begin to play with the sand feeling it fall through their fingers. Tell them there is an imaginary bucket of water next to them, which they can mix with the sand to make castles. Encourage them to think about the shape they have created. Is it decorated with shells? Has it got more than one tier? Is there a moat around it? Ask individual children to describe their castles and then invite children to move around the room admiring each other's work. Ask children to choose a partner and return to one of the castles. The children decide who is going to be the builder and who is going to smash the castle. Talk the children through the story as they dramatise: 'Once there was a girl building a sandcastle. She mixed her sand very carefully and moulded the castle . . . Then her brother came along, knelt down to look at the castle . . . and smashed it!'

- Practise this again so that the 'smashed it' moment is a **freeze frame**. Encourage the children then to sit down and together compose the story of why the brother chose to smash the castle. Compare stories and then ask the children to recite the poem to each other, using either 'sister' or 'brother' as the first word.

- Direct children to write down or draw their version of why the castle was smashed, perhaps working in groups to devise a strip cartoon.

Becoming a poet

- Direct the children to draw around their open hands or bare feet using a faint pencil line.

- Ask the children to imagine a situation where they have used their hand or foot to destroy something. For example, it might be when they have stamped upon a spider. Encourage them to use the pattern of the poem in order to make a new one perhaps modelling yourself, for example: 'Spider, with this hand I made a claw and tore your web. I am sorry. What can I do to make it better?'

- Encourage children to refine their poems, perhaps in pairs, then write them around the outlines of their hands or feet. They will need to space words carefully in order to border the image. As this can be tricky an alternative is to write within the borders of the outlined foot or hand.

- Alternatively, the children can use Textease (www.softease.com/) in order to shape their poem electronically.

How it worked in the classroom

This work was taught by two teachers of parallel Year 2 classes. This enabled them to model the roles of the brother and sister described in the poem and act out the event.

Initially, the image of the poem was introduced using a smartboard so that all the children had an immediate and enlarged image to relate to. Not surprisingly, the initial discussion focused on their personal experiences. Children realised that holding up your hand could be culturally grounded; for example, asking a question in class or stopping for the open palm of the 'lollipop lady'.

After a teacher had read the poem out loud to the class, the children experimented with making fists and adopting angry, shocked or disappointed expressions. Working in pairs, the children were asked to tell personal anecdotes, describing in detail an occasion when they had done something bad with their hands. Although most children were eager to share these memories with their peers, some of them were more reticent and became silent, when their teacher approached to listen to the stories. The teachers recognised that their presence affected some children's willingness to relate their innermost thoughts and feelings. This situation changed as soon as the teachers shared their own misdemeanors. Children

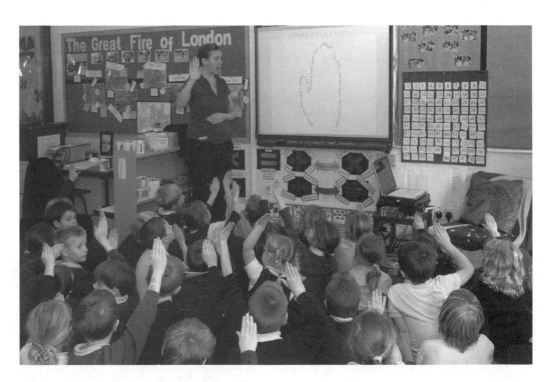

Plate 6.1 Teacher modelling performance.

began spontaneously to share the positive things their hands had done and this was encouraged. With permission, some children told their partner's story.

Returning to the poem, the children practised a shared reading, supported again by the smartboard image. The children made suggestions about how the poem might be spoken. For example, one child pointed to the comma and demonstrated how to incorporate a meaningful pause into his reading aloud. Returning to their talk partners, the children worked on memorising the poem and reciting it, while using their fists and facial expressions to emphasise the words. While the children practised performing the poem with actions, one child suggested saying the second part of the poem with hand on heart to signify that they were truly sorry. Once the children felt confident enough to recite the poem without the written words, they presented it to others. The performances concluded with the children reflecting on different interpretations and their effectiveness.

During the drama, the school hall became the seaside setting for sandcastle building while a background soundtrack of waves and seagull cries supported the **visualisation**. Children were encouraged to write their names in the 'sand' and crunch it between their bare toes.

Following the 'making' of the sand castles, children were invited to admire each other's and comment on them. One child described their castle as being 'like a hotel', while another was proud of their pyramid of towers complete with a drawbridge.

Plate 6.2 Imagining writing names in the sand.

Plate 6.3 Freeze frame.

The time that the children spent perfecting their castles made destroying them more powerful; children's belief was such that they appeared genuinely upset when this happened, as was evident in the **freeze frame** captured in Plate 6.3. Following this, further **freeze frames** were produced to recreate the children's alternative 'hand' stories; for example, a story describing the breaking of a favourite toy.

When the children came to write their own shape poem, the teacher modelled her own thinking as she wrote, before providing the children with a simple writing frame:

_____ , with this hand I _____
I am sorry.

_____

Once the children were happy, they were given a hand template and invited to publish their work.

Anna and Robert (Figure 6.3) thought carefully about patterns on the page, spacing their words carefully so they took on the shape of the hand.

Anne and Robert chose stories from their own memories. Although the words are different, both writers capture the poignancy of the original poem. The succinct

Figure 6.3 Anna and Robert's work.

nature of Hegley's work enables the children to tell a story from salutation ('Friend') to problem ('I pushed you in the prickles'), through apology ('I am sorry') to resolution ('Let me take them out').

Related objectives from the Primary Framework for Literacy for Year 2

Speaking

Explain ideas and processes using imaginative and adventurous vocabulary and non-verbal gestures to support communication.

Listening and responding

Respond to presentations by describing characters, repeating some highlight and commenting constructively.

Drama

Adopt appropriate roles in small or large groups and consider alternative courses of action.

Creating and shaping texts

Draw on knowledge and experience of texts in deciding and planning what and how to write.

Related poems

If you want to follow the theme of behaviour, then an appropriate poem is 'Bully for you', also by John Hegley (2002). This encourages children to tell someone if they are being bullied, and the repetition in the poem makes it easy to memorise and use as a model.

If you are following the theme of shape poems, then 'The Shape I'm In' by James Carter (2002) is a humorous poem that uses words as **calligrams**; for example, 'w i d e as a smile'. Children can make **calligram** words using mixed media and word processing.

CHAPTER 7

Really looking

As a teacher, I remember arriving at school one morning to find that there had been an unexpected heavy frost. The bright sunshine illuminated the irridescent coating on the surrounding countryside and tempted me to abandon my timetable and venture outside with my class. The children, armed with imaginary cameras, began to focus on the many beautiful sights: a huge piece of ice torn from a puddle and held up like a pane of glass against the light; a beech tree rimed with frost silhouetted against the red sun; fields of frozen grass and spiders' webs encrusted with diadems. The children returned to the classroom, capturing the moment by writing in **free verse**. The poems were returned to time and again as the experience was relived through their published and well-loved anthology, which eventually fell to bits through frequent use.

This was the age when creative writing was a priority in schools. Children were encouraged to write from first-hand experience, and this was often preceded by the close observation of natural forms or phenomena. Simply having a box of interesting things for children to look at closely, sometimes with magnifying glasses – a starfish, a sea horse, a lump of crystal or dried flowers – would form the stimulus for a poem. There is much to recommend this approach to writing, where children need to sharpen their senses in order to record a memory of a particular object. This can be extended into metaphoric thinking: what does an object look like? What does it remind you of? Young children are often excited by comparisons, as they are an important part of the symbolism that underpins their fantasy play. Taking the children for a walk around the locality to find things that look like other things can be an introduction to metaphor. A line of telegraph poles can look like a line of soldiers, pampas grass like witches' hair, waving branches like arms and a hollow tree like an open mouth.

The slide in Figure 7.1, from a PowerPoint presentation, demonstrates how a village walk provided a creative opportunity to explore figurative language in the context of a **multi-modal** narrative. Creativity has always been an important part of education, and this is recognised in current guidance:

Teachers found that when they actively planned for and responded to pupils' creative ideas and actions, pupils became more curious to discover new things for themselves, were open to new ideas and keen to explore those ideas with their teacher and others.

(DfES, 2003: 31)

The yew tree in the garden was like a big green umbrella and it was cool and dark underneath – a witch's cave.

5

Figure 7.1 Multimodal text of children's words and pictures with clues for the reader as to what images will appear on the next slide, in this case telegraph poles.

In his poem 'Snail', Ted Hughes makes some close observations of what the snail *is*: ('wrinkled'), but also what it is *like* ('a whale'). There are some wonderful metaphors: 'a ribbon of sea' for the snail's trail and 'God's kiss' for the touch of the snail's soft body.

Snail

With skin all wrinkled
Like a whale
On a ribbon of sea
Comes the moonlit snail.

The cabbage murmurs:
'I feel something's wrong!'
The snail says 'Shhh!
I am God's tongue'.

The rose shrieks out:
'What's this? O what's this?'
The snail says: 'Shhh!
I am God's kiss.'

So the whole garden
(Till stars fail)
Suffers the passion of the Snail.

(Hughes, 2001)

Paving the way

In order to engage with the poem, the children may benefit from first-hand experience of snails. For example:

- Have some snails available in the class for children to observe closely. Black paper placed in the bottom of the snail's tank should make their trails more obvious. This resource could be available for a few days before you start work on the poem.

- Encourage the children to use an observation book to record what the snails look like and what they do: eat, leave trails and so on. These observations can be returned to when the children begin to write their own poems.

- Alternatively, provide a pad of Post-it notes® for children to write down words or phrases that arise from their observations, such as 'pin-head eyes'. These could be stuck to a display board near to the tank of snails and used to support poetry writing.

Meeting the poem

- Ask the children if they like snails. Why? Why not? Ask them for words that they think describe snails. Can they think of similes or metaphors in addition to the ones that the poet uses? Is there anything that snails remind them of? Are the children frightened of snails? Why? Why not?

- Read the poem to the children. If you have an additional adult working with you, share the reading perhaps with one person reading the words 'spoken' by the snail, the cabbage and the rose.

- Using an enlarged version of the poem, ask the children what parts of the poem they like and why. Discuss anything that the children might struggle with, such as the phrase 'Suffers the passion'.

Performing and presenting

- Choose children to be the cabbage, the rose and the snail. Be the narrator yourself, but encourage the chosen children to speak the three parts. These lines could be highlighted on an IWB to support reading.

- Organise the children into groups, each with their own paper copies of the poem. Provide highlighters so that they can mark up the text for a prepared reading of their own.

- Allow time for the children to practise before performing to each other. Support the children as they analyse their own work and that of their peers. Consider what makes a good reading. Does it help to memorise their lines? Does movement support the performance? Are some lines more effective when read by more than one person?

Reading, writing and reflecting

- Organise a drama session where the children are invited to be cabbages. This may involve the children making a suitable **freeze frame** or sitting on the floor in rows. We cannot assume that children automatically know what a growing cabbage looks like. Their knowledge of cabbages may not extend beyond its often unappetising appearance on a dinner plate. You may wish to make a collection of cabbages to demonstrate the different varieties. As the children freeze frame as cabbages you may want to support them by asking: 'Are you a small cabbage with tight leaves? Are you a curly-leafed cabbage?'

- Tell the children that when you click your fingers or clap your hands you will be the hungry snail (**teacher in role**). Fortunately, you do not need to slither along the ground to do this, but you might wish to adapt your voice to suggest the slippery predator as you say, for example, 'Mm this cabbage looks so green and juicy; perhaps I should nibble one of its leaves'. As you move in role between the cabbages, encourage the children to speak their thoughts out loud (**thought tracking**). Children might say, 'Oh no, don't eat me I'm much too tough!' Follow this with a class discussion; did they imagine that the snail ate them or did they have a lucky escape?

- Ask the children who they think is more afraid of the snail: cabbages or roses? Discuss the reasons behind their responses. If the children are puzzled by this question, put forward the likelihood that the roses in the garden are less afraid of snails because their thorns discourage them from crawling up their stems. Invite the children to consider how the cabbages might protect themselves. This introduces **problem solving**. Children could team up with a partner to decide how to solve the problem. Encourage inventive solutions such as using drawing pins, slug pellets and nets, or building a moat. Children could draw and label diagrams of these solutions using paper or screen. This may support their thinking and deepen their commitment.

- As **teacher in role**, walk through the cabbages. Again, children can use **thought tracking** to speak their thoughts, although this time they may comment on the ways in which they have protected themselves. This can be followed by class reflection. Did their solutions work? Did the snail leave them in peace or not?

- Produce a letter written by you as a gardener. Share this with the children. The letter might reveal that the gardener is writing to a company that specialises in poison pellets. His intention is to kill all minibeasts – slugs, worms, beetles and so on – as he is tired of them eating many of the plants and vegetables that he grows.

- Organise a **conscience alley** where the gardener wrestles with his conscience; one side of the alley tries to persuade him not to kill the animals. These children could take on the role of minibeasts. The opposite side of the alley tries to persuade the gardener to destroy the minibeasts. These children could adopt the roles of the gardener's family or friends, who want to eat the cabbages, and the shopkeepers he supplies, who want to sell them. The gardener needs to walk inside the alley and listen carefully to the opposing points of view. Encourage the children to think of real reasons why he mustn't act in a particular way. For example, the bee could say: 'Please gardener, don't poison the garden, you'll have no honey if you kill me!', whereas the shopkeeper might say, 'I won't buy cabbages with holes in from you'. Encourage the children to add weight to their arguments by adapting their voices and adding appropriate actions. Following the **conscience alley**, the gardener must consider his decision and explain which arguments were most persuasive. The opposing sides can then swap in order to argue a case from another perspective. Out of role, the class could discuss this dilemma and its relevance to their lives. Rural children may hold different opinions to pupils from urban areas.

- Making a recipe for something that will protect the cabbages but not harm the snails could be an appropriate activity with which to close the drama. The teacher might suggest magic dust to protect the cabbages, which doesn't harm the snails. Pairs of children could then make the dust and **mime** spreading it carefully over the garden around the cabbages. Alternative ideas might be forthcoming from the children and these could also be mimed.

- Find other poems about minibeasts, both real and imaginary.

Becoming a poet

- Take the children for a walk and encourage them to find things that look like other things. Take photographs and publish a class book, which is an illustrated story of their walk. This will give the children experience of using figurative language – important for poetry writing.

- Use the cabbage, rose or snail as a starting point for a shared or guided poem. Having chosen one of the subjects, use key words and develop similes and or metaphors, such as 'the rose smells like my auntie's perfume', or 'the rose is a frilly skirt'. Once the children have made a collection of this kind they can select their preferred phrases to create a poem. For example:

> The cabbage is like a football
> Its leaves as green as my baby sister's eyes
> When it rains it drinks up the raindrops
> And sleeps in a bed!

- Writing **riddles** could encourage the children to begin to think metaphorically. Model how to write minibeast riddles by underlining how the poet needs to describe their subject without naming it. If you are writing snail riddles, return to the descriptive words and phrases described in 'paving the way'. For example:

> I leave a trail of silver,
> I take my house wherever I go,
> What am I?
> > *A snail*

> I wear yellow and black jumpers,
> I hum as I work
> What am I?
> > *A bee*

How it worked in the classroom

As our visit to the classroom coincided with the drama activities linked to the poem, the teacher was keen to involve us. The school hall became a court room and Linda took on the **high status role** of a judge.

In role, she produced a letter from a mistle thrush who was concerned that the use of insecticides on snails would lead to a lack of food for her and her fledglings. The children were invited to put their point of view to the judge with due consideration to her important position. The children's comments were interesting and informed and included points of view in favour of pesticides, for example, 'I'd rather have people kept alive rather than snails; we can always wash chemicals off our

Plate 7.1 Meeting Linda in role as the judge.

Plate 7.2 Performing poetry by heart.

food'; and points of view against pesticides, for example, 'If you use chemicals on cabbages you would kill other animals as well as snails'. The 'judge' listened to all points of view, summed up and concluded the drama with a vote.

Later, the children performed the poem. It worked best when the children spoke their lines from memory. Trying to read and perform is too difficult for young readers.

The children pictured performing in Plate 7.2 had learned the lines and so were free to use expression and movement effectively. Later, when the class were asked what activities they had most enjoyed, the drama activities and the performance were firm favourites.

The riddle writing was demonstrated and modelled by the teacher who then supported independent writing.

Oliver spent a lot of time composing and illustrating his riddle. His previous observational work clearly supports his writing. Looking closely enabled him to use words like 'slimy' and 'wrinkly'. Discussion enlarged his vocabulary to include scientific terms such as 'antennae'; his research supports his knowledge and

Figure 7.2 Riddle by Oliver, aged 6.

understanding of behaviour ('I come out at night'), and the penultimate line, 'Farmers think I'm a pest', links directly to the drama debate. There is also clear evidence of analogous thinking in the line: 'I am similar to a slug'.

Related objectives from the Primary Framework for Literacy Year 2

Speaking

Speak with clarity and use appropriate intonation when reading and reciting texts.

Explain ideas and processes using imaginative and adventurous vocabulary.

Listening and responding

Listen to others in class, ask relevant questions and follow instructions.

Respond to presentations by describing characters, repeating some; highlight and comment constructively.

Group discussion and interaction

Listen to each other's views and preferences, agree the next steps to take and identify contributions by each group member.

Drama

Adopt appropriate roles in large or small groups.

Present . . . work . . . for members of their own class.

Understanding and interpreting texts

Explore how particular words are used, including words and expressions with similar meanings.

Engaging with and responding to texts

Explain their reactions to texts, commenting on important aspects.

Creating and shaping texts

Draw on knowledge and experience of texts in deciding what and how to write.

Make adventurous word and language choices appropriate to the style and purpose of the text.

Related poems

'Snail', by John Drinkwater (1987) is a short poem that focuses on the snail's shell, and could lead to a closer look at this creature's 'house'.

'The Caterpillar' by Christina Rossetti (1987) is a poem that supports a consideration of the caterpillar's predators.

'The Cabbage White Butterfly' by Elizabeth Jenkins (1987) is something of a protest poem, as it speaks out against those who catch butterflies in nets.

'Bee' by Emily Dickinson (1987) is a short poem written as a letter to the bee from the fly. This might stimulate children to use this model to write a letter poem from one minibeast to another.

'Who's That Tickling My Back?' by Ian Serraillier (1986) is a short action poem easily recited by two voices, and one that the authors have used with many young children.

CHAPTER 8

Silly stuff

There is a wonderful plethora of humorous verse for children. Some masters of this genre come instantly to mind, such as Michael Rosen, Spike Milligan, Benjamin Zephaniah and Kit Wright. Humorous verse can engage children who are otherwise ambivalent to poetry, and such poetry often makes a serious point. Colin McNaughton's poem 'Are we nearly there yet?' comes to mind, which simply repeats the two lines: 'Mummy are we there yet, / Are we nearly there?' (McNaughton, 2000) so that they 'fall off' the margin of the page, indicating the infinity of a rant that tortures parent drivers. Zephaniah (1994) has wonderful, rootsy work such as his poem 'Talking Turkeys', but underlying the humour in this poem are messages about imprisonment, genetic farming and cruelty. Other poets cleverly celebrate the absurd, such as Brian Moses, an imaginative and humorous poet whose work begs to be read aloud. As a musician he is very aware of the sound quality of his poems, which have their own unwritten score. There is an excellent opportunity to hear his work, and that of others, on the Poetry Archive (www.poetryarchive.org). At this site, children are able to hear the poet's voice and their unique interpretation.

The poem 'Walking With My Iguana' has a wonderful rhythm and metre and the poet's recitation cleverly uses pauses, tone of voice and speed to animate the work. It is easy to underestimate how cleverly wrought this poem is unless it is heard with the musical accompaniment that Moses adds. It tells the story of someone who takes their iguana for a walk in the incongruous setting of an English seaside town.

Walking With My Iguana

I'm walking
with my iguana

I'm walking
With my iguana

When the temperature rises
to above eighty five,
my iguana is looking
like he's coming alive.

So we make it to the beach,
my iguana and me,
then he sits on my shoulder
as we stroll by the sea.

and I'm walking
with my iguana

I'm walking
With my iguana

Well if anyone sees us
we're a big surprise,
my iguana and me
on our daily exercise.

Till somebody phones
the local police
says I've got an alligator
tied to a leash.

when I'm walking
with my iguana

I'm walking
With my iguana

It's the spines on his back
that make him look grim,
but he just loves to be tickled
under his chin.

And I know that my iguana
is ready for bed
when he puts on his pyjamas
and lays down his sleepy head.

And I'm walking
with my iguana

still walking
With my iguana

With my iguana . . .
with my iguana . . .
and my piranha

and my chihuahua
and my chinchilla
and my gorilla
my caterpillar
and I'm walking . . .
with my iguana . . .
with my iguana . . .
with my iguana . . .

(Moses, 2000)

Paving the way

- Show the children images of iguanas using high-quality photographs. Encourage them to search for their own images and to think of words to describe them.

- Explain that you are going to share a poem about someone who takes an iguana for a walk. Let them consider what this might entail in terms of the likely reactions of passersby and in terms of practicalities such as the need for a lead. It is likely that they will want to discuss why someone might want to take an iguana for a walk and this may lead to sharing similar stories. For example, there is a man in the village where I live who can often be seen crossing the road with a green parrot on his shoulder.

- Seat the children in a circle and let them take turns to imagine taking a creature for 'a walk' in the **performance space**. They will need to consider how they will carry or lead their creature depending on its size and temperament, and how they will need to demonstrate this by pulling, pushing, stretching up high to lead an elephant, or bending down low to lead a caterpillar. This game can be a lot of fun and could be extended to include the whole class moving together. Once everyone joins in children and their 'pets' can interact. This supports reluctant performers, who then share the walk in relative obscurity.

Meeting the poem

- Encourage the children to use their drumming fingers, stamping feet or unpitched instruments to copy the rhthym of the poem. There is the opportunity to add several beats after 'And I'm walking' and before 'with my iguana'.

- Using the Poetry Archive website, introduce the poem by listening to Moses read his work. Encourage the children to join in with their percussion.

- Focus on the vocabulary of the poem and discuss any interesting words such as 'grim'.

- Listen to Moses read the poem again and encourage the children to visualise the incident. The children may find it helps to close their eyes. Afterwards they might compare their images. The poem suggests a very hot day ('above eighty five'), so what do they imagine was happening on the beach whilst the iguana was taking a stroll? Children could draw their imaginings and compare.

- Demonstrate to the children how to use the strategy of **hot seating** in order to question the owner of the iguana. If the children are unfamiliar with this strategy you could provide some starter questions, such as: 'What do you feed your iguana on? Where did you get him from?' Direct children to make up their own questions and take turns to sit in the hot seat as the iguana's owner.

- Additionally, children could take turns to be hot seated in role as the iguana. In this way children could explore the poem from the iguana's point of view. You could ask questions such as: 'Do you like walking with your owner? What do passersby do when they see you? Do you mind being on a leash?'

- Focusing on the verse that describes a bystander's telephone conversation with the police, encourage children to work in pairs to recreate the conversation and consider what each character might say in these circumstances. Telephone conversations, which do not draw on body language or eye contact, can easily be recreated by seating pairs of children back to back, perhaps with the support of props such as mobile phones.

- Eavesdrop on the telephone conversations, then recount some of what has been said; for example: 'Do you know I heard a lady saying that she had seen the iguana frighten a Rottweiler!' In this way the teacher shares children's work without the need for them to perform to others. Alternatively, invite children to improvise their telephone conversations for others to hear.

Presenting and performing

- Encourage the children to perform the poem by giving each group a verse to memorise. Each group then performs their part, with the whole class joining in the chorus and percussion. The last verse, which tails away as a list of exotic creatures, could be given to individuals to perform a line each. If the children are unsure about these creatures they can research them using the internet.

- By dividing the class into two, each half can work on producing different presentations to perform. Each group then has the opportunity to both observe and take part in a performance. This supports reflection and critical response.

- A **tableau** can be an interesting backdrop to a recitation. This could be in the form of a beach scene, where children's poses subtly change as they react to the iguana being taken for a walk.

Reading, writing and reflecting

- Let the children adopt the role of a bystander telling the story of the incident described in the poem to someone who wasn't there. This could be paired or group work and lead to children writing individual or group recounts.

- As **teacher in role**, tell the children the story from a bystander's point of view. For example, you might imagine being an ice cream vendor, a lifeguard or a concerned holidaymaker. Model how to write this story as a letter or postcard to a friend, family member or the local council. The bystanders could all have different points of view. The ice cream vendor, for example, might be delighted with an increase in trade brought about by crowds of bystanders anxious to see an iguana.

- Draw or paint pictures or make three-dimensional models of unusual or fantasy animals, complete with a lead.

- Read, practise and perform other humorous poems about unusual animals.

Becoming a poet

- Demonstrate to the children using an enlarged copy of the poem, on the IWB, how some words can be changed without affecting the rhyme scheme. For example, the poem could become 'Walking With My Crocodile', and lines such as 'when he puts on his pyjamas' could become 'when he puts on his bed socks'. Give children individual copies of the original poem to modify themselves. Children can then practise reading their adapted poems to each other.

- Alternatively, the children can use their fantasy pictures to write a **kenning**. These are simply poems that describe something without using its proper name. This encourages children to think carefully and use language economically and powerfully. For example:

Scaly stalker,
Slow walker,
Sun lover,
Lazy lizard
      Iguana

Peanut cracker,
Banana peeler,
High swinger,
Nit picker,
      Cheeky monkey

How it worked in the classroom

By the time we visited the children, an elaborate collage of an iguana was 'walking' across a display board surrounded by photographs of these exotic creatures.

During our visit, the children all demonstrated walking their own personal 'iguanas', while a recording of the poem provided a rhythmic accompaniment. The children's movements demonstrated how well they had internalised the rhythm of the poem. In a limited space a class could do this as two groups, which would provide an opportunity for diffident children to watch others. Building on the children's **visualisation** of the beach scene, the teacher used groups of children to **freeze frame** activities at the beach and then asked them to adapt these to show

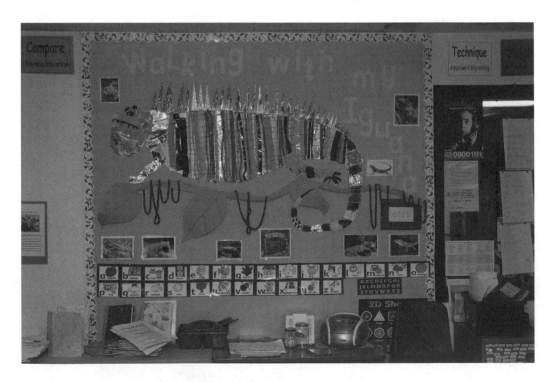

Plate 8.1 Using art and design to engage with the poem.

before and after pictures. For example, a group of children chose to make a frame of eating a picnic on the beach. After imagining seeing someone walking an iguana, they changed their poses. Some of the group froze with their mouths open and imaginary food halfway to their lips, while some stood and pointed. These frames were then shared with the other groups and discussed.

In the class we visited, the teacher supported the children's initial **freeze frames** by using headlines enlarged on an IWB. These included the intriguing 'Heatwave Hits Hastings as People Hit Beach'. Children could devise their own headlines to match their **freeze frames**.

To explore thoughts and feelings, the teacher set up a **gossip alley**. She used tape to designate the floor area, which focused the children's attention on their working space. Using the alley as a path for one child to walk their iguana, she divided the remaining children into two groups of bystanders, inviting them to take up their positions along the taped lines. The children were then asked to say out loud what they thought or felt (**thought tracking**) as the iguana passed by. Children were reminded that they could use the tone of their voice to suggest their fears, concern or surprise and gesticulate if they wished. Working in this way supported inclusion as voices and **asides** merged and children were able to make an extended response such as: 'I don't think an iguana should be allowed on the beach!' or simply: 'Wow!'

After the teacher had modelled **hot seating** the iguana owner, she chose to divide the class into groups of five or six. One child was invited to take the 'hot seat' whilst the remaining children asked questions **in role** as bystanders. Although

Plate 8.2 Gossip Alley.

Plate 8.3 Jan observes group hot-seating.

there were a number of children talking simultaneously, this enabled more children to ask and answer questions, supported reticent speakers and kept everyone focused. Organising the class in this way provided an excellent opportunity for adults to observe and assess children whilst still enabling them to provide support when necessary.

Related objectives from the Primary Framework for Literacy Year 2

Speaking

Speak with clarity and use appropriate intonation when reading and reciting texts.

Tell real and imagined stories using the conventions of familiar story language.

Listening and responding

Listen to others in class and ask appropriate questions.

Respond to presentations by describing characters, repeating some highlight and commenting constructively.

Group discussion and interaction

Ensure that everyone contributes, allocate tasks and consider alternatives and reach agreement.

Work effectively in groups by ensuring that each group member takes a turn challenging, supporting and moving on.

Drama

Adopt appropriate roles in small or large groups and consider alternative courses of action.

Present their own stories for members of their own class.

Understanding and interpreting texts

Draw together ideas and information from across a whole text.

Give some reasons why things happen or characters change.

Engaging with and responding to text

Explain their reaction to text, commenting on important aspects.

Creating and shaping texts

Draw on knowledge and experience of texts in deciding and planning what and how to write.

Make adventurous word and language choices appropriate to the style and purpose of the text.

Select from different presentational features to suit particular writing purposes on paper and on screen.

Related poems

'Blue Macaw' by Roger McGough (2004) describes the challenges of owning a macaw kept in a bottom drawer. While this poem is humorous, it also hints at the cruelty of captivity.

'There's an Awful Lot of Weirdos in our Neighbourhood' by Colin McNaughton (1987) is an anthology full of funny poems about bizarre people and their strange habits.

'My Praying Mantis' by John Lyons (1994) is a poem set in the Caribbean. The poem is about keeping a pet insect and carrying it on one's shoulder, lest it gets eaten by the neighbour's cat. Which it does.

'My Brother Bert' is a hilarious poem written by Ted Hughes (1988) that describes Bert's menagerie of exotic pets and the problems that they cause.

CHAPTER 9

Key questions

Why listen to poetry?

Children are fortunate if they enjoy hearing rhymes and jingles read or recited from an early age. Without the voices of more experienced language users, young children's poetry experiences would be limited by their inability to read. Listening to others read or recite poetry frees our imagination to focus on enjoying the experience, comprehending what is being said without the need to decode. Some rhymes do not necessarily need to be fully understood. For example, consider this playground chant:

> Eena meena
> macka racka
> rare ra
> dominnacker
> chickerbocker
> lollypopper
> om
> pom
> PUSH.
>
> (Traditional, Anon.)

What does it mean? It hardly matters, as it's fun for the tongue and useful when choosing who's going to be 'it' in a game of chase. However, if a poem challenges our understanding, then listening to the poem read by someone who reads fluently and expressively may support us.

Everyone needs to listen to poetry read aloud, even the most able readers. Could you imagine reading music without ever listening to it? How much would we miss?

Having attended memorable poetry readings by poets such as Michael Rosen and Brian Patten, I am able to carry elements of their unique voices in my aural memory. When I read their poems out loud to children, students or myself their voices echo in my head and subtly improve my renditions. Inviting poets into school to work alongside your class is an excellent opportunity for children and adults to listen to the poet's own voice. Alternatively, websites such as the Poetry Archive (where you can access poetry read by the poets themselves) or CDs can be used. Another way to hear poetry read by a variety of voices is to utilise the school community. By persuading people, young or old, male or female, to read or recite poetry using their personal dialect, accent and interpretation, teachers provide opportunities for children to become discerning listeners.

In the Primary Framework for Literacy (DfES, 2006), strand two refers to listening and *responding*. The explicit inclusion of responding underlines the active nature of listening. We rarely listen without experiencing some response, even when responding means we elect not to continue listening.

Why is it important to learn poetry off by heart?

It is important for the teacher to learn poetry off by heart because we can present poems more powerfully, making eye contact with our audience as we recite. In pre-literate societies poetry was often shared in this way as a community experience and then handed down, and altered, through the generations.

It is possible to gauge the reaction of our audience if we can actually see them, rather than having to read and recite simultaneously. Reading from texts on the IWB can be good for drawing attention to language features, but the first time children hear a poem it is better to recite it to them so you can more confidently play with speed, tempo and pitch in response to your audience. You are demonstrating how well it can be done, and children are keen to copy. Fortunately, poetry is memorable, and so easier to learn than other texts. It is often figurative and so the pictures it creates stay in our imagination and the rhythms linger with us too. In this way, visual and aural aspects explore the ways in which meaning is made, and we have both aspects to hand more easily if we have the poem off by heart.

Being able to draw from a rich inner repertoire of poetic forms makes writing poetry so much easier.

Why talk about poetry?

When we talk about poetry, we are formulating our own opinions and personal responses to a poem's subject matter, language, imagery and pattern. We raise questions in our minds that cannot always be answered immediately or simply. It is useful therefore, in the first instance, for a teacher to model this 'talking' to themselves (sometimes referred to as a 'metacognitive approach') as in the following example. This poem might work well as an addition to the Year 1 block of work relating to the senses, as described in Chapter 3.

Giants upstairs

The stormy sky turns black as night
And the forked lightning flashes
As if a giant who needed light
Was striking enormous matches.

From the clouds comes the sound of thunder
As if we had giants upstairs
Who were moving monster furniture
And knocking over tables and chairs.

In the rain above the town
It thunders louder than before
Like a giant falling down
And rolling over and over along the floor.

(Cook, 1982)

Having read the poem twice out loud, the teacher could say:

I think this poem is about a bad storm as the poet includes the words thunder and lightning. It reminds me of a few weeks ago when I was in my house and the sky got very dark and we had to put on the lights although it was only the afternoon. I wonder why the poet talks about giants and calls the poem 'Giants Upstairs'? Maybe the poet talks about the giant's knocking over things to help me to imagine how powerful and noisy the storm is and how much damage storms can do. Giants would make a lot of noise with their enormous feet. The poet uses similes comparing a flash of lightning to the sudden striking of a giant match. When I read the poem I picture giants in my house. In my head they look a bit like Hagrid, the giant in the Harry Potter films, but he may be too kind a giant to imagine being like thunder. Perhaps I should picture the giants like the one in our *Jack and the Beanstalk* book, he's much scarier. Giants can be scary and so can storms . . .

When we model talking about poetry, we quickly recognise that doing so often requires subject specific language, such as the term 'simile' in the above example. This suggests that children cannot talk about poetry without this knowledge, but they can and do invent their own unique language with which to convey their ideas, often to the amazement of adults. However, it is part of our role as teachers to empower children by giving them appropriate tools for the 'job'. If teachers model the use of language to talk about poetry, children can be further empowered to enter discussions.

If we are talking with others, we may argue our point of view, perhaps altering our opinion in the light of what others say. We may feel able to hold fast to our opinions when others disagree, or we may back down believing our understanding to be limited. With an additional adult in the classroom we can model a paired discussion about a poem, making sure that we demonstrate both agreement and disagreement. Some useful phrases may be: 'How interesting; I hadn't thought of that before', 'I'm not sure I agree with you because . . .' or 'Why do you say that?' This can develop into children's paired or group discussions, where an adult can observe or facilitate the talk and children can learn from each other. The sooner this stage can be reached the better, as Nash *et al.* (2002) remind us: 'Where teacher talk is the main medium of transmission the child is effectively excluded from learning, to the frustration of both child and teacher.'

Of course, it is crucial that talk is animated, reflecting curiosity and wonder and not leading to tedious over-analysis. Not every poem needs to be discussed. There should be opportunities for silent response, as I found to my cost when asking a six year old to tell me what he thought of a poem immediately after hearing it. 'Long!' was his explicit reply.

Can poetry help children with EAL learn English?

In learning another language, it is important that we have the opportunity to listen to the new language being spoken. We need to hear the sounds and their groupings, which may not be like our first language. We must also master different intonation patterns and understand how these relate to meaning. Listening to and learning poetry is an ideal way to do this, as there is often an emphasis on sound groupings in terms of rhyme, alliteration and assonance. Understanding and performing poems gives the opportunity to experiment with intonation in order to express meaning. Even a simple rhyme such as:

> Pease pudding hot
> Pease pudding cold
> Pease pudding in the pot
> Nine days old
>
> Some like it hot
> Some like it cold
> Some like it in the pot
> Nine days old

> (Anon.)

gives the child learning English a chance to add actions such as stirring the pudding or holding up nine fingers for the days. The facial expression can reflect pleasure or disgust at pease pudding hot or cold, and in this way the unwritten aspects of language can be understood and expressed. The sound groupings include alliteration: ('pease' and 'pudding'), and rhyme: ('old' and 'cold') and the stressed syllables are 'hot', 'cold', and 'old' – we learn to stress the ends of the first, second and fourth phrases.

Riley suggests that, for pupils who have English as an additional language, 'written language in the form of stories, rhymes and poetry promotes spoken language through offering rich linguistic models for the child' (2006: 207). Spoken language generated from the simple rhyme 'Pease Pudding' could include a description of what pease pudding actually is and what foods children like hot or cold. The form of the poem could be used by inserting words from the child's first language; for example, 'Samosas hot, samosas cold . . .'.

It is important to remember that the child learning English may already be used to learning extended texts in their own language off by heart, including sacred readings, often written in poetic language. In this command of language they may be more advanced than their monolingual peers.

Why write poetry?

In teaching young children to write, we have to include as many text types as possible in order for them to be fully literate. There are challenges in mastering all forms of writing. In trying to construct a story, for example, we have to hold the whole form in our memory so that we can develop the plot and characters, which requires a stamina difficult for young writers. In writing a report we have to make sure that the factual information is correct, which requires research and checking.

Poetry has its own demands but in some ways is easier than other forms. As a poet we can take great risks, even inventing our own words and spellings. Punctuation, form and length are decided by the writer and many poems are short, memorable and easy to hold in the head as we plan the next word, phrase, line and verse. Children can achieve the whole form quickly and then have time to revise and edit.

In writing, children are using what they know about poetry and the way it works and they have a real purpose for enlarging their vocabulary in terms of poetic language. Figure 9.1 shows an example from a student teacher of work in progress where pupils are using an image of the sun. First, they collect words as 'spokes', and then work on the form within the red 'sun'.

Young poets have a real context in which to understand how the language works in terms of alliteration, rhyme, assonance and other linguistic features, and they are able to express complex ideas or personal experiences with a minimum of

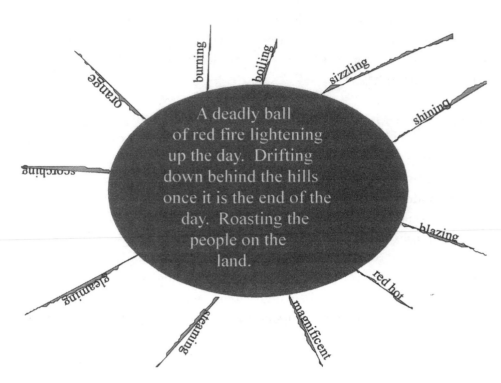

Figure 9.1 Work in progress.

words. Writing down our thoughts can help us to understand them. In writing poetry, children have increasing opportunities to use multimodal forms. Helping young writers is complex: 'Poetry needs to be rolled around the mind and tongue, given air and space, if it is to satisfy the writer' (Bearne, 2002: 107). Bearne is making the point here that writing poetry is not always quick and easy. Words need to be considered, recited, reviewed in order to select and order the best. She suggests:

> On the one hand, teachers want to encourage individuality of voice, choice of subject and preferred form; on the other hand poetry in the classroom can be all too easily reduced to exercises in using powerful adjectives.
>
> (2002: 107)

Powerful adjectives? Powerful verbs? Powerful nouns? Powerful writing is surely not just about individual words but the sophistication of their fusion; the dance they perform with other words, phrases and stanzas. Bearne makes the point that poets chose words as part of a troupe.

Scaffolds may be helpful and support the Vygotskian approach, which influenced the original National Literacy Strategy Framework (DfES, 1998) with its continuum of shared, guided and independent work. We suggest scaffolds in the form of writing frames, but Bearne herself warns that scaffolds can become 'prisons', restricting children's voices and preferred forms of writing.

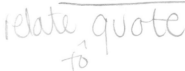

relate quote
to

Published poets would be unlikely to use scaffolds, but they have their own inner repertoires of remembered phrases, stanzas and longer works, which influence their writing. It would be inconceivable for anyone to attempt to write poetry if they had not heard or read examples, preferably a rich variety of different forms. Teachers can organise this. Organisation rather than teaching is required, as it is important to encompass children's choices; texts can be brought in from home or chosen from a wide selection in the class, including playground rhymes and jingles, popular songs, jokes, puns and other forms of language play. Simply reading a poem from an anthology and then asking 'Who would like to take this home and find your favourite?' can result in children choosing thoughtfully and being able to talk about their choices. Writing in the style of an author can follow from this and here the teacher can play a key role in modelling writing.

The following poem was written by a teacher and her class of Reception, Year 1 and Year 2. She shared with the children 'Each Peach Pear Plum' by Allan and Janet Ahlberg (1989) and the children identified the many fairytale characters hidden in the illustrations. The teacher gave the children the line 'Each sock, sandal, shoe' and then asked them for ideas for the next line.

> *Each sock, sandal, shoe,*
> I spy Little Boy Blue
> *Little Boy Blue in a box*
> I spy Goldilocks
> *Goldilocks in the night*
> I spy Snow White
> *Snow White eats a bun*
> We see everyone.

The italicised lines are the ones she gave as prompts. In describing the work, she said:

> I knew this wouldn't be easy and I wanted to focus on children's listening skills so that they heard the line in their heads before we wrote it. I didn't write the poem down until we'd finished it. I chose the scaffold line carefully with a character in mind and the children could discover and practise the rhyme themselves before suggesting it. We had great fun drawing the new pictures with hidden characters and our publication has almost fallen to bits the children have read and re-read it so much.

Haiku, limericks, rhyming couplets can easily form scaffolds of specific forms but if children are to practise their own voice in their own form they can graduate to freer forms of poetry, often simply with help in editing.

Jennifer was taken to study a river as part of cross-curricular work and then given the first line of the poem 'Oh How I Love the River' as a stimulus. Originally the poem was written as prose, but the teacher helped her to edit it into a more conventional poetic form including removing the prompt. Jennifer was supported by the first-hand experience of seeing the river and helped with editing, but it is her experience of poetry that is the important prerequisite. This enabled her to use near rhyme, alliteration and repetition:

> The river rushing
> Boulders mushing the soft mud together
> Silver fish go dashing past at the last minute of the day
> Time for bed for me and you
> But not for that rushing river.

As Bearne argues, 'it is the heard and felt experience of poetry which is the starting point for the risky business of writing' (2002: 108).

Why use ICT to teach poetry?

Technology is increasingly being used in the classroom and it has an important part to play in the teaching and learning of poetry. Finding poems is easy using a search engine, and if there is a particular poem that you are anxious to find but

Plate 9.1 IWBs can help by projecting large-scale versions of poems.

can only remember part of then the Poetry Library offers an efficient service that will search for you.

IWBs can help by projecting large scale versions of poems; it is possible to superimpose these on selected screens. In the example in Plate 9.1, the teacher has superimposed 'Rhyme' by Elizabeth Coatsworth, (featured in Chapter 3) on top of a digital image downloaded from the internet. She is able to draw children's visual attention to print easily and underline, omit or emphasise words and phrases.

Poets themselves can be researched using the internet, and there are some exciting examples of poets reading their own work at sites including the Poetry Archive and talking about their work at sites including Booktrust. Children can also download digital images as backdrops for their own work.

For example, Robert wrote a poem in response to a class study of the 'Lady of Shallot'. In deciding how to present his work he did an online search to find a suitable picture in Google Images. For a detailed explanation of how to do this see King and Pagett (2006).

Word processing can support presentation and help in composition by allowing us to cut and paste verses that have repeated lines or structures. The following poem is adapted from 'When I Grow Up' by Colin McNaughton (1990):

> When I grow up
> I would like to be
> Eating toast and jam
> For tea [original verse]
>
> When I grow up
> I would like to be
> A sailor on the
> Bright blue sea [child's verse].

Simply cutting and pasting the first two lines gives children a simple structure to work with. Children can choose their own font style and size to suit the meaning of the poem.

Colour, imported images and creative spacing can help to make shape poems. The example in Figure 9.2 is from work by a student teacher.

The writing is supported by the image. Colours are used and the poem teases us by flying around making us turn the page as we read.

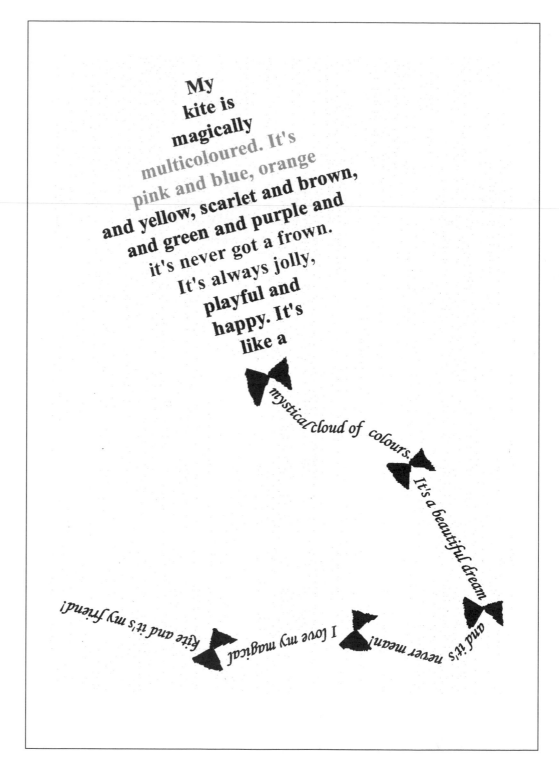

Figure 9.2 Concrete (shape) poem.

Why make cross-curricular links?

Poets write about anything and everything. They write about what they know well and about what they don't fully comprehend in order to gain a deeper personal insight. The subject matter and range of emotions are diverse and boundless. So poetry in school may be constrained if taught as simply part of English. It makes sense for teachers of young children to make connections between poetry as part of the Primary Framework for literacy and poetry that supports our appreciation and understanding of the wider curriculum. This may include what is sometimes referred to as the 'hidden curriculum' – namely personal, social, moral and spiritual issues. Although in this book we focus on the teaching of poetry linked to the proposed units of work as outlined in the Primary Framework, we believe that the suggested activities make direct links to other areas of the curriculum. While the children engaged in Hughes' poem 'Snail' (see Chapter 7) extended their scientific knowledge and understanding of a snail – its habitat, appearance and diet – they were also challenged them to consider the ethics of pest control.

Psychologists such as Vygotsky clearly accept that children learn by moving from what they know to what they don't yet know by making connections. This can be compared to completing a jigsaw. Sometimes we find two or three pieces that fit easily together, while at other times we search for a long time to find one piece which, when discovered, enables another piece to fall neatly into place. The more we repeat a puzzle, the more likely we are to see the connection between each piece, the easier the jigsaw becomes and the quicker the whole picture is revealed. Learning can be like this.

Let us return to the earlier example of Cook's poem, 'Giants Upstairs'. On hearing this poem we might think about the scientific phenomena of storms drawing from our geographical or scientific knowledge and understanding. We might make connections to other texts about giants: illustrations, stories, films, adverts or music. We may have a strong emotional response to the poem, depending on our first-hand experience. If we have experienced a severe flood or hurricane our responses may be extreme – physically as well as emotionally.

Why read poetry?

Children may have a repertoire of poems from hearing chants, jingles and more serious works read by others. However they need to read poetry for themselves as well as hear it being read. Reading aloud allows them to experiment with presentation, playing with intonation, pitch and tempo in the most meaningful form to them. Reading aloud in a group can be supportive for struggling readers as they are able to tackle texts they are unable to read independently.

Reading also teaches children that poetry can be written in many forms including **concrete poems**, thin poems, short poems and **free verse**. Illustrations are often important; I am thinking here of Charles Keeping's dramatic pen and ink drawings, which support the Alfred Noyes poem 'The Highwayman' (1981) and Ahlberg's 'Each Peach Pear Plum' (1989) both awarded the Kate Greenaway medal. In such texts, the reader makes meaning from the words and pictures. Other graphic features are also important. Text is often enlarged emboldened or manipulated by the poet in order add emphasis and persuade us that the text should be read in a certain way.

If we are to analyse a poem, we need a printed version to hand in order to scan and skim for particular language features that may be difficult to hold in the memory, and annotating printed texts can be a useful.

Children's understanding of phonics is supported by reading. They may learn, for example, that 'gnat' and 'naughty' are alliterative, or that 'rhyme' and 'time' share the same rime but different letter strings. In reading for ourselves we are able to read at our own pace, savouring particular words and phrases, perhaps reading and re-reading as we respond to the work. Reading poetry for themselves can help young readers to progress in their fluency because anticipation and prediction are supported by rhyme, repetition and rhythm. The poets themselves push us into well-informed guesses about the next word, phrase and stanza.

Why connect poetry with the arts?

We have already considered the relevance of making links between poetry and the wider curriculum; however, poetry also has particular affinity with other art forms. It is our optimistic view that the Primary Framework, with its explicit reference to drama, speaking, listening and responding, will strengthen the teaching of the arts.

Art forms are complementary. While children make a collage of an iguana in art and design, experiment to find a sound most like thunder with musical instruments, practice moving like a dragon around the school hall through dance and question a gardener about his use of pesticides through drama, they inhabit the poem in question. Through the arts, children can explore a poem – its setting, period, characters and mood – in the social context of their classroom. This demands sharing ideas and drawing from previous experience. When we approach poetry in this way, we are providing an inclusive learning environment in which all pupils can access and experience poetry.

 Effective learning is an active process, and a combined arts approach supports a response to poetry through visual, aural and kinaesthetic approaches. When the Year 1 children working on Tony Mitton's poem 'The Bag' began to ask why no one visited the house described in the poem, they were able to answer their question through **improvisation**. Before they set off to explore the 'house', which was actually a designated area of the empty school hall, their teacher invited them to consider what they could see, hear and feel. Afterwards, when the children recalled the experience, one six year old described seeing dark and dusty portraits. Such is the power of drama that other children confirmed this.

Why perform poems?

Poetry invites response. Benton and Fox (1985: 19) make the point that 'meaning is a compound of what the poem offers and what the reader brings'. We cannot respond without imagination. It is important that pupils are given opportunities to live in their imagination and to respond critically. Pagett and Somers suggest that, 'although poems need to be heard and teachers play an important part in reading them to pupils, there is no guarantee that anyone other than the good auditory learner is learning anything, or even listening' (2005: 4).

There are many ways of encouraging children to respond to poetry, such as discussion, drawing, painting and drama, which we have described in our work in schools. Responding through performance is powerful because it can support the kinaesthetic learner – those who learn by doing. Performers need to learn the poem off-by-heart, and this in itself gives them an intimacy with the work, as active engagement enables us to personalise our learning and place it into a meaningful context.

While children consider how best to present poetry to others, they need to revisit the poem, and this may result in a deeper appreciation and understanding. How will they convey the mood of the poem? Will the presentation be more meaningful if supported by visual images, **costume** or a musical accompaniment? These are important questions for which children will have numerous and sometimes conflicting answers. Arriving at a consensus will necessitate discussion and decision making, and may require adult mediation.

Performance is a chance to experiment with different voices and movement so that the performer is not only engaged with the meaning but also fashions the meaning for themselves and then persuades us, the audience, that it is so. For instance, the poem 'Dragon' cited in Chapter 4 can be performed as a narrative of what happened when the performer saw a dragon, followed by another performer repeating the same words as an incredulous response: 'You saw a dragon . . .'.

Performance can give children mastery over poetic form. They are making the poem their own and understanding that the words written on the page are not living until they connect with their interpretation and response. Performing is inclusive, as reluctant readers or writers may well be the best performers and this can challenge the able language user, which is not always easy. While they devise and practice their performance, children work collaboratively, criticising each other's work, experimenting and modifying what they are doing in a community of performers.

When the decisions have been made and the performance is over, the effect on both the audience and the performers can be powerful. It is noticeable how some children's confidence and self-esteem increases as a direct result of preparing and presenting. Furthermore, it is often those children who find aspects of school difficult who rise to the challenge on these occasions.

Children will frequently respond to a performance spontaneously and honestly: 'I was shaking when I started but then I felt good when everyone clapped at the end. I missed out a bit, but think I got better.'

Further discussion, where positive criticism and questioning is both modelled and encouraged, often develops understanding. This was demonstrated during our work in schools when groups of children devised different presentations of the same poem. When they commented on their performances compared to others, they were able to consider how best to convey the qualities of the poem.

Poetry performance is fun. It is social, it is collaborative and it is inclusive.

Glossary

Acrostic

These poems are written around the initial letters of a key word, often at the beginnings of lines, as in the acrostic in Chapter 5.

An aside

Children speak in character and add an aside, which demonstrates their true feelings. Children need to appreciate that an aside is often a stage whisper, and has to be audible to the audience while still sounding whispery.

Calligram

A calligram can be a poem, phrase or word in which handwriting or typeface is an important part of the focus. For example, a poem about a ghost might be written in a 'shaky' font.

Concrete poem

This is a poem that forms a picture or follows the contours of a shape. The shape of the poem adds to the poem's meaning.

Conscience alley

The children stand in two lines facing each other and represent two opposite arguments; they voice their opinions as a child or adult walks down the 'alley' between them. This can be an effective strategy, particularly if the children use movement to emphasise their points. Afterwards, the person walking the alley can be invited to describe their reactions to the arguments that they heard and consider whether or not they were persuaded by them.

Costume

Although young children appear to revel in dressing up, adopting the role of a character does not need to involve sewing a whole-scale wardrobe. Signifiers that support characterisation such as hats, ears or tails, together with simple **props** such as spades, umbrellas or walking sticks, can contribute to belief and add visual appeal for an audience without detracting from the real work in hand.

Emotional alley

As for conscience alley, but the focus is on the children expressing their thoughts and feelings about the central character's behaviour.

Free verse

This appears very much like prose, as it is written without the constraints of rhyme, yet it retains the succinct nature and pattern of poetry, both as it is written and when it is spoken.

Freeze frame

Individuals or groups devise a still image of a person, animal or situation, rather like a photograph or a sculpture. Participants need to focus on how they convey meaning through facial expressions, body position, levels at which they are working and distance from others. Freezing action in this way supports concentration and develops a quality response. This technique can also support class management, as the children need to focus on their interpretation while remaining still. Freeze frames can also be used to convey the passage of time; for example, children may depict a scene five minutes before a key moment and then five minutes after.

Gossip alley

As conscience alley, but the two lines of children simply speak out loud their reactions to the central character and the situation.

Haiku

A poetic form from Japan that has three lines and seventeen syllables in the pattern of 5–7–5:

> The star fish is mine,
> It smells of the salty sea,
> And now it is dead.

Hot seating

An adult or child in role can be asked to sit in the 'hot seat', where they will be asked questions by others who might be in or out of role. Questions can be considered before the activity, or an adult can model the technique in order to stimulate ideas. Hot seating can involve an entire class, or smaller groups could be set up if this gives children more confidence (as in Chapter 8).

By using this technique, children can explore a character in depth, questioning their feelings, attitudes, motives and actions. Of course, the same character portrayed by different children is likely to answer questions differently, and this provides important opportunities for children to consider their own interpretations of people and events.

Imaginative play or role play
This refers to the kind of spontaneous play in which children engage when they adopt the role of someone or something other than themselves. In this way, they are able to take part in imagined events either independently or with others. Adults can support this play by providing areas to represent – for example, a shop or an airport, although children will often be inventive with an upturned chair or a cardboard box.

Improvisation
This builds directly from imaginative role play, and involves adults and children spontaneously 'making up' how they react, move and speak without a script. For example, children visiting the empty house in Chapter 4 improvised collecting things to put into an imaginary bag.

Intertextuality
This refers to the way in which texts are related, for example in terms of setting, structure or parody. Many traditional tales make links to others in this way through settings such as a dark wood, characters such as a wicked step-parent or themes such as abandonment.

Kenning
These were originally old English or Norse poems. In them something is described without mentioning its name. Trusty blade or Chest tickler for example might describe a sword. Kennings can be written as simple two word lists and alliteration can be used as in our examples in Chapter 8.

Masks
Masks can be used to enhance performance and help audiences relate to a child in role. This can be effective particularly when children are taking on the roles of animals or mythical creatures. Some children may enjoy the anonymity that masks appear to provide, while others may feel restricted by them. For oral performances half-face masks work best, as they leave mouths free to project sound freely. This kind of mask would work well for 'Rumble in the Jungle' as in Chapter 2; however, many children are familiar with wearing face paint, and this can be an effective alternative.

Mime
This refers to using action to demonstrate what you might be doing and feeling without the use of props or speech; for example, miming taking an iguana for a walk as suggested in Chapter 7.

Multi-modal texts
This term refers to texts that are produced using more than one mode; for example, children may represent ideas through written text and illustration, or they might use a PowerPoint alongside an audio recording.

Performance/presentation

When children perform they may do this to a small audience of one, a group, a class, the whole school and/or parents and carers. Performance might involve an initial sharing of ideas, or it may be the result of several rehearsals. It is important that a child's perception of performance is broad and that the process of devising drama is valued as much as the final product. Young children need to experience performing to a variety of audiences and should not be rushed into presenting in a formal setting too soon. It is important that children are able to give and accept critical responses to their performances and adapt their work in the light of this. This will need to be modelled in the first instance.

Performance space

This can be any designated area that you and the children feel is appropriate. It is to some extent dependent on the formality of the performance and the size of the audience. While you work within a class context, a circle is a good standby as it provides an inclusive area where everyone can see and be seen. This builds on the format used for many drama games and has links to traditional storytelling. When performing to a larger audience, such as another class or parents and carers, a more theatrical approach can be taken by using a stage or raised drama blocks.

Physical theatre (white mime)

This technique involves using the body to devise an inanimate object or objects such as a chair or a bowl of fruit. This can be extended by adding movement. For example, a child freezing as a fire could start to move their fingers to represent flames; two children portraying a gate could use their arms to demonstrate how it opens and closes. A group of children working with the poem in Chapter 5 used parts of their bodies to represent the tail, ears and feet of a dragon, which was then brought to life through movement and sound.

Problem solving

The children are given a dilemma to discuss and resolve. This may be tackled verbally or be explored by writing and drawing, as suggested in Chapter 7. Problem solving can be undertaken while in or out of role.

Props

See **Costume**.

Riddle

A riddle presents a form of word puzzle. Several descriptive clues support the reader in solving the puzzle by the end of the poem.

Role play

See **Imaginative play or role play**.

Soundscape

Children can use their voices, body percussion or untuned instruments to create a soundscape or background to enhance their poetry performance. In the work relating to the thunderstorm in Chapter 3, children worked on an the sound of a rain shower. A soundscape of the beach could introduce the poem 'Walking my Iguana' in Chapter 8, whilst an eerie soundscape could set the scene for a performance of 'The Bag' in Chapter 4.

Tableau

This can be created when children devise a freeze frame, to which more and more characters are added until a tableau is formed. The tableau can then be brought to life using a known prompt, such as a cymbal crash or a simple click of the fingers. This strategy can demonstrate action taking place over a period of time, as in cabbages growing in a garden or people arriving at a beach.

Teacher/child in role

This refers to an adult or child adopting the persona of someone or something they are not. This might mean changing one's appearance by the use of simple props or signifiers, such as a hat or walking stick, or merely changing one's voice and gait as the teacher did when adopting the role of the iguana owner in Chapter 8. While in role the adult or child is able to talk to, question, challenge or request advice and help.

High status role

An adult adopts a figure of authority or importance. In this way the adult can lead the class, give orders and be in firm control (see the judge's role in Chapter 8).

Middle status role

An adult adopts a role of equal importance to the children's roles. In this way the adult and the class share ideas and support each other.

Low status role

An adult adopts the role of someone needing help, support and guidance. This may appear to be the most risky status, as control is handed over to the children; but it can work well if the children are engaged.

A teacher may be in role while the children remain themselves or both the teacher and the children may work in role together. For example, in Chapter 8 we describe a teacher adopting the role of the man walking an iguana while the children take on the roles of bystanders.

Thought tracking

This strategy allows children to speak out loud their own thoughts while in role. This can be done quietly for the teacher's benefit or loudly for the whole group or class to hear. The teacher can use this technique during improvisation by stopping the action and choosing certain children to voice their thoughts. Alternatively, individuals in freeze frames could be invited to do the same.

Visualisation
This strategy can support children in creating or recreating visual images. An adult acts as facilitator by talking through a scenario in order to support children's imaginative pictures. Children often find that it helps to close their eyes while they listen to an adult voice; background music or sound effects can also be effective supports. Visualisation can be followed by children describing and drawing what they have seen or recording their images on paper or screen.

White mime
See **Physical theatre**.

References

Agarth, J. (1986), *Say it Again Granny! 20 Poems from Caribbean Proverbs* (London: Bodley Head).

Ahlberg, A. and J. Ahlberg (1989), *Each Peach Pear Plum* (London: Picture Puffins).

Andreae, G. (1996), 'Rumble in the Jungle', in *Rumble in the Jungle* (London: Orchard Books).

Anonymous (traditional rhyme), 'Pease Pudding', in Opie, I. and P. Opie (1951), *The Oxford Dictionary of Nursery Rhymes* (Oxford: Clarendon Press).

Balaam, J. And B. Merrick (1987), *Exploring Poetry 5–8* (Sheffield: NATE).

Barrie, J. M. (1911), *Peter and Wendy* (Hodder & Stoughton).

Bearne, E. (2002), *Making Progress in Writing* (London: Routledge).

Bennet, J. (1987), *Noisy Poems* (Oxford: Oxford University Press).

Benton, M. and G. Fox (1985), *Teaching Literature 9–14* (Oxford: Oxford University Press).

Booktrust, available online at www.booktrusted.co.uk.

Brown, R. (1981), *A Dark, Dark Tale* (London: Anderson Press).

Carter, J. (2002), 'Vacuum Cleaner', in *Cars Stars Electric Guitars* (London: Walker Books).

Coatsworth, E., 'Rhyme', in Bennet, J. (1987), *Noisy Poems* (Oxford: Oxford University Press).

Cook, S. (1982), 'Giants Upstairs', in *The Poem Box: More Poems for Younger Children* (London: Blackie & Son).

Cook, P. (2000), *The Works: Every Kind of Poem You'll Ever Need for the Literacy Hour* (London: Macmillan).

Department for Children, Schools and Families (n.d.), *The Standards Site*, available online at www.standards.dfes.gov.uk/primaryframeworks/literacy/planning/Year1/Poetry (accessed 1 October 2007).

DfEE (1999), *The National Curriculum for England* (London: DfEE).

DfEE (2000), *Curriculum Guidance for the Foundation Stage* (London: QCA).

DfES (1998), *The National Literacy Strategy* (London: DfES).

References

DfES (2001), *The National Literacy Strategy Framework for Teaching* (London: DfES).

DfES (2003), *Excellence and Enjoyment: A Strategy for Primary Schools* (London: DfES).

DfES (2006), *The Primary National Strategy, Primary Framework for Literacy and Mathematics* (London: DfES).

DfES (2007), *Early Years Foundation Stage* (London: DfES).

Dickinson, E. (1987), 'Bee', in A. Harvey (ed.), *Of Caterpillars, Cats and Cattle: Poems About Animals* (Middlesex: Viking Kestrel).

Drinkwater, J. (1987), 'Snail', in A. Harvey (ed.), *Of Caterpillars, Cats and Cattle: Poems About Animals* (Middlesex: Viking Kestrel).

Drury, R. (2007), *Young Bilingual Learners at Home and School* (Stoke on Trent: Trentham Books).

Foster, J. (2004), *Dragon Poems* (Oxford: Oxford University Press).

Google Images, available online at http://images.google.co.uk/.

Hardy, B. (1977), 'Narrative as a Primary Act of Mind', in M. Meek, G. Barton and A. Warlow (eds), *The Cool Web* (London: Bodley Head).

Hegley, J. (2002), 'Untitled', in *My Dog is a Carrot* (London: Walker Books).

Honeysett, M. (1998), 'When There's a Fire in the Jungle', in R. McGough (ed.), *The Kingfisher Book of Comic Verse* (London: Kingfisher).

Hughes, T. (1967) *Poetry in the Making* (London: Faber & Faber).

Hughes, T. (1988), 'My Brother Bert', in *Meet My Folks* (London: Faber & Faber).

Hughes, T. (2001), 'The Snail', in M. Morpurgo (ed.) *Because a Fire was in My Head* (London: Faber & Faber).

Jenkins, E. (1987), 'The Cabbage White Butterfly', in A. Harvey (ed.), *Of Caterpillars, Cats and Cattle: Poems About Animals* (Middlesex: Viking Kestrel).

Kelly, A. (2005), 'Poetry, Of Course We Do It. It's in the National Curriculum: Primary Children's Perceptions of Poetry', in *Literacy*, 39 (3).

Kenward, J. (1998), 'Dragon', in G. Morgan (ed.), *Read Me: A Poem For a Day of the National Year of Reading* (London: Macmillan).

King, J. and L. Pagett (2006), 'Poetry Gallery', in *The Primary English Magazine*, 11 (5).

Lyons, J. (1994), 'My Praying Mantis', in J. Agard and G. Nichols (eds), *A Caribbean Dozen* (London: Walker Books).

Matthews, M. (1994), 'I Love', in G. Nichols and J. Agard (eds), *A Caribbean Dozen* (London: Walker Books).

McGough, R. (1983), *Sky in the Pie* (London: Kestrel).

McGough, R. (2003), 'The Sound Collector', in *All the Best* (London: Puffin).

Macmillan, I. (2000), 'Ten Things You Find in a Wizard's Pocket', in P. Cook (ed.), *The Works: Every Kind of Poem You'll Ever Need for the Literacy Hour* (London: Macmillan).

McNaughton, C. (1987), *There's an Awful Lot of Weirdos in Our Neighbourhood* (London: Walker Books).

McNaughton, C. (1990), *Who's Been Sleeping in My Porridge?* (London: Walker Books).

McNaughton, C. (2000), *Wish You Were Here and I Wasn't: A Book of Poems and Globe Trotters* (London: Walker Books).

Medwell, J., D. Wray and R. Fox (1998), *Effective Teachers of Literacy* (Exeter: University of Exeter, for Teacher Training Agency).

Mitton, T. (1998), 'The Bag', in *Plum* (London: Scholastic).

Moses, B. (2000), *I Wish I Could Dine with a Porcupine* (London: Hodder Wayland).

Moses, B. (2000), 'Walking With My Iguana', in *Behind the Staffroom Door: The Best of Brian Moses* (London: Macmillan).

Nash *et al..* (2002), in G. Thompson and H. Evans (2005), *Thinking it Through: Linking Language Skills, Thinking Skills and Drama* (London: Fulton).

Nichols, G. (2005), 'I Like to Stay Up', in *Everybody Got a Gift* (London: A. C. Black).

Nichols, G. and J. Agard (eds), *A Caribbean Dozen* (London: Walker Books).

Noyes, A. (1981), *The Highwayman* (London: Oxford).

Pagett, L. and J. Somers (2004), *Off By Heart* (Sheffield: NATE).

Patten, B. (2001), 'A Small Dragon', in M. Morpurgo (ed.), *Because a Fire was in My Head* (London: Faber & Faber).

Poetry Archive website, available online at www.poetryarchive.org.

Poetry Library website, available online at www.poetrylibrary.org.uk/queries.

Pope, J. (2007), 'Our Visit to the Zoo', in J. Forster (ed.), *My First Oxford Book of Animal Poems* (Oxford: Oxford University Press).

Rawsley, I. (2000) 'Sounds', in *The Works: Every Kind of Poem You'll Ever Need for the Literacy Law* (London: Macmillan).

Riley, J. (2006), *Language and Literacy 3–7* (London: Paul Chapman).

Rosen, R. (1981), 'This is the Hand', in *You Can't Catch Me* (London: André Deutsch).

Rossetti, C. (1987), 'The Caterpillar', in A. Harvey (ed.), *Of Caterpillars, Cats and Cattle: Poems About Animals* (Middlesex: Viking Kestrel).

Serraillier, I. (1986), 'The Tickle Rhyme', in R. McGough (ed.), *The Kingfisher Book of Comic Verse* (London: Kingfisher Books).

Smith, F. (1971), *Understanding Reading: A Psycholinguistic Analysis of Reading and Learning to Read* (London: Holt Reinhart & Winston).

Smith, W. J. (2001), 'The Toaster', in M. Harrison (ed.), *A Book of Very Short Poems* (Oxford: Oxford University Press).

Tennyson, A. L. (1986), *The Lady of Shalott* (Oxford: Oxford University Press).

Textease website, available at www.softease.com.

Toczek, N. (1997), 'Dragon' and 'The Dragon in the Cellar', in *Dragons Everywhere* (London: Macmillan).

Winston, J. and M. Tandy (2001), *Beginning Drama 4–11* (London: Fulton).

References

Wright, K. (1987), 'The Magic Box', in *Cat Amongst the Pigeons* (London: Viking Kestrel).

Zephaniah, B. (1994), *Talking Turkey* (London: Viking Poem), available online at www.benjaminzaphaniah.com/rhymin.html.